# Queen Square Bristol

ANDREW KELLY

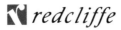 *redcliffe*

First published in 2003 by Redcliffe Press Ltd,

81g Pembroke Road, Bristol BS8 3EA

Telephone 0117 973 7207

ISBN 1 900178 84 2

British Library Cataloguing-in-Publication Data

A catalogue record for this book is available from the British Library.

Design, typesetting and new photography by Stephen Morris Communications, smc@freeuk.com, Bristol and Liverpool,
and printed by HSW Print, Tonypandy, Rhondda.

## Acknowledgments

Many people have been of help in this project. Funding for this book was provided by Bristol City Council. I would like to thank them, and especially Helen Holland, for this support. I would like to thank also Chris Heath, Alastair Brook, Jon Brett, John Sansom, Jonathan Banks, Barry Taylor, Tina Speake, Stephen Price, Sheena Stoddard and the ex-residents of Queen Square who answered questions. Also thanked is Melanie Kelly who edited the book. We are grateful to those owners of copyright materials for permission to reprint materials and use illustrations. If we have failed to acknowledge any copyright holder please contact the publishers and this will be rectified in any future editions.

# Contents

# Foreword ■

As you walk around Bristol (and it is a city experienced best on foot) you will at some point reach Queen Square. Once home to Bristol's wealthiest citizens – and before that a civic space used for bowling, grazing and the disreputable pursuit of bull baiting, when it was known as the Marsh – Queen Square is now mainly occupied by offices. After 150 years of decline it is at last being returned to its original eighteenth-century magnificence. The transformation is remarkable – the result of years of effort and dedication by those who love Bristol. Although lively at times with arts events, Queen Square also offers that haven of peace and quiet all cities need. City workers eat their lunch sitting in the shade of ancient plane trees, or teams of boule players compete along the gravel walkways, or crowds listen to jazz. On many days, and at night, the square provides a vision of civic beauty – a word that we have tended to discard when discussing urban places, but there is no better description. Robert Browning could have been thinking of Queen Square when he wrote:

> Had I but plenty of money, money enough and to spare
> The house for me, no doubt, were a house in a city square.
> Ah, such a life, such a life, as one leads at the window there!

As well as being the city of bridges and churches, Bristol is the city of squares. Queen Square is the largest of these, in fact the largest urban square outside London where only Lincoln's Inn Fields beats it. By 1718, as Queen Square was in its second decade of development, St James's Square had been completed and construction had begun at Orchard Street (actually a square). In 1720, Dowry Square was started. Fifty years later, King Square and Brunswick Square were still being built. In 1790, the first plots of land that would eventually create Portland Square were being sold. Others, such as Clifton's Victoria Square, were to follow well into the nineteenth century. In 2000, they were joined by Millennium Square, part of At-Bristol.

There is no doubt that some of these squares are more remarkable in terms of architecture than Queen Square. But when its history, design, housing, landscaping and the great statue of William III are taken together, Queen Square is the most important of them all for what it tells us about Bristol, good and bad, and how it helps us to understand the past, and plan the future of the city.

I first came across Queen Square soon after I started work in the city in 1993. By that time cars were no longer allowed full access except around the perimeter, so I do not remember the dual carriageway being used, though the road was still there. For years afterwards, I saw the square every day, as my bus took me round it as it headed out of the centre. I did not know the full story of the square then – and did not, in fact, till I finished work on this book.

What struck me most, and continues to strike me now, is the size of the square. I had never seen an open space this large at the heart of an English city. It remains for me one of the glories of Bristol, the place where visitors are always taken and who gaze, just as I did, in wonder. Since then, I have read much about the history of the square, seen the square change, and sometimes returned just to sit and watch. Most of my meetings mean that I walk through the square daily, and even when a quicker route is available, I confess that I often make a detour. As I talked with people about this book, I was delighted to discover that they do the same.

The Czech novelist, Ivan Klima, wrote in 2002: 'To love a city is to know its history, to know the fates of its outstanding citizens, to know not only its famous churches but also its little corners, its parks, its hidden secrets.'[1] This short book attempts to provide a view of one small part of Bristol: the life and times of Queen Square.

# Queen Square in Bristol

QUEEN SQUARE is half a mile from Temple Meads Station, close to the Bristol Old Vic theatre and surrounded by the Floating Harbour. To the south is the River Avon and The Grove; to the west, Prince Street and Narrow Quay, the city centre, Canon's Marsh, Wapping Wharf, Harbourside and College Green; to the east, Redcliffe and St Mary Redcliffe Church; and to the north, the historic heart of the city including King Street, the city's first suburb built outside the medieval walls.

# Introduction

QUEEN SQUARE has been a place for assembly and ceremony, living and working, art and leisure, riots for democratic reform and, allegedly, capital punishment. The square was built in the early eighteenth century when Bristol was emerging as England's second city. Within a century, the complacency that past success can engender meant that the city was beginning to fall behind newly industrialised cities like Birmingham, Liverpool and Manchester. In the 300 years since it was built, Queen Square has, like much of Bristol, suffered the economic and political vicissitudes of the times. Now, at the beginning of a new century, the renovated square takes its place at the heart of a city confident about its future.

# The Origins of Queen Square ■

QUEEN SQUARE started as the Marsh, a piece of wetland owned by the city, with ancient title granted by King John II to the Burgesses of Bristol (though Bristol technically did not become a city until the 1540s, functionally it was a city from the start). Following the creation of the new channel for the River Frome in 1247, the topography of the Marsh was changed. The port was improved, with new fortified walls created near to where King Street is now and gates built providing access to the Marsh. This was a place used for wrestling, the grazing of animals, bull baiting and, it has been said, the execution of pirates. A bowling green was created in 1622. Shooting practice and ceremonial weapon-firing took place there. Gunpowder was stored. The Marsh was also the place for the viewing platform – a timber scaffold – where Queen Elizabeth watched the three-day mock battle led by armour-plated soldiers staged on the river and in Wapping Wharf that was the expensive culmination of her stay in Bristol in August 1574. [2]

Interest on a donation of 100 marks made in 1610 and rent from butchers allowed to graze cattle were used to pay labourers to maintain the site. Despite the area being intensively used, the corporation allowed refuse dumping there.

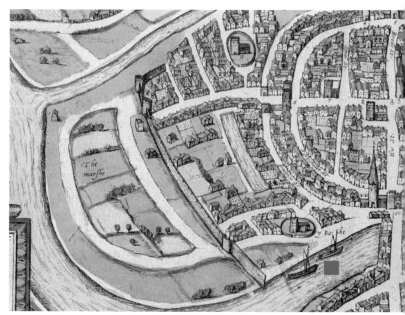

**The Marsh from Brightstone**, 1640. George Hoefnagle.
[Bristol Museums & Art Gallery]

This became a public scandal although rubbish was still being dumped in 1706, when the square was being built.

The Marsh played a role in the civil war of 1642-1646. Bristol declared for Parliament and both sides fought hard to capture the city, recognising that it was impossible to control the West Country without its support. Batteries were set up

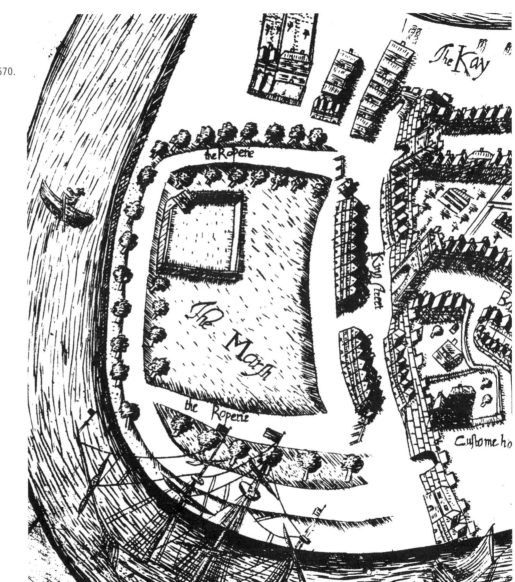

*The Famous Citie of Bristoll*, c.1670.
James Millerd.
[Bristol Museums & Art Gallery]

on the Marsh prior to the siege of Bristol in 1643 to defend the Quay and the city suffered badly, being occupied by Royalists and Parliamentarians in turn. It was not until 1656 that the Marsh was reinstated as a public space, but the corporation reserved the right to use the area for elections or for training volunteers. The green was described as 'nice' and 'surrounded by a stone wall' by the Dutch artist William Schellinks when he visited Bristol in 1662.[3] Celia Fiennes, in Bristol in 1668, said 'just by the water side is a long rope yard which is encompass'd with trees on either side which are lofty and shady, therefore its made choice of for the Company of the town to take the diversion of walking in the evening; this compasses round a large space of ground which is called the Marsh, a green ground.'[4] Maps dated 1670 show that the Marsh was planted with trees. Two years later, in another map, a bowling green and lodge (built in 1660), cattle and cannon were marked. In 1698, a ropewalk was added where ships' halyards were woven and tied between elm trees to dry.[5]

Detail, *The Citty of Bristol*, 1684. James Millerd. [Bristol Museums & Art Gallery]

Bristol was an important centre for shipbuilding in the seventeenth century, though it was illegal to carry out this trade on the Marsh as launching slips damaged the banks (the council did allow some shipbuilding when a payment was made to the city). Samuel Pepys, during his visit to Bristol in June 1668, saw a ship being built in the Key – 'a most large and noble place' – where later he walked, saw the Custom House at Welsh Back, and went through Marsh Street.[6]

By the start of the eighteenth century, Bristol was second only to London for commerce, and trade with the Americas and West Indies was booming. Industrial growth was led by the production of iron, glass, bricks, pottery and other goods demanded by the 'New World'. In addition to trade in products made in the city, Bristol was a regional centre embracing not just the south west, but also South Wales and the area north of Bristol to Bridgnorth. Trade was also strong with Ireland.[7] At this time there was a local population of around 20,000; only London and Norwich were larger. Daniel Defoe said Bristol was 'the greatest, the richest, and the best Port of Trade in Great Britain, London only excepted'.[8] Indeed, it was the competition with London, and the wish to emulate the capital, that was partly behind the push by Bristol Corporation to build Queen Square.

*An Exact Delineation of the Famous Citie of Bristoll*, 1671. James Millerd. [Bristol Museums & Art Gallery]

# The Building of the Square ■

PROVINCIAL CAPITALS were trading centres, with ports, cultural facilities and civic and political administrative functions, according to Peter Borsay. The urban renaissance that followed the Restoration of 1660 and the adoption of the Dutch style of architecture, was marked by 'the renewal and transformation of the landscape',[9] with one of the most important features being the construction of city squares.

The first English square was in Covent Garden, finished in the 1630s. It was developed by Inigo Jones. In the late seventeenth century, residential squares were developed in London with St James's and Bloomsbury Squares in the 1660s, and Golden Square and Red Lion Square in the period 1670-1680.

The main inspiration for Queen Square seems to have been Lincoln's Inn Fields, completed in the seventeenth century. Most of these developments were intended for the wealthy who were interested in elegance, recreation and conspicuous consumption: a new lifestyle of formal display and stylised routine was to typify the age, rewarding commercial prudence and good fortune. Thus the Marsh, used for casual leisure and boat building, became a place for the new merchant élite. It was to be another 300 years before it was used widely by the public again.

Queen Square is considered to be the first residential square built outside London. One commentator says that Queen Square 'combined the fashionable open space with the fashionable shaded walk, apparently the first residential square in England to do so'.[10]

The development of King Street between 1650 and 1665, together with some building on Narrow Quay (then known as Wood Key) led the way to the development of the Marsh, just as Queen Square helped the development of the adjacent Prince Street, The Grove and Welsh Back. It took some years for building to start. The council noted a minute at its meeting in 1669 instructing the city surveyors and mayor to look at the Marsh and identify 'persons willing to accept leases therein for five lives' at a rent of '12d per foot at the least for frontage.'[11] Nothing happened. CFW Dening, whose book *The Eighteenth Century Architecture of Bristol* was published in 1923, believes that the delay was due to fears that the scheme would mean the end of use of the square as a civic space and 'fashionable rendezvous'. It would also mean an end to the grazing of livestock and the destruction of the bowling green.[12] Given the opposition that this would have created, it is not surprising that there was a delay.

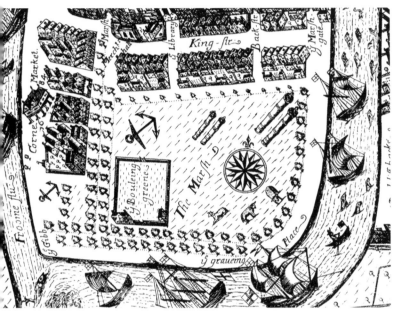

*The Citty of Bristoll*, 1673-1684. James Millerd.
[Bristol Museums & Art Gallery]

By the end of the seventeenth century, according to Bristol historian Timothy Mowl, the council was in financial trouble. John Romsey, the long-serving town clerk (with the exception of 1688, he held the post from 1676 to 1720), along with the mayor, John Bachelor (involved in the drapery business) proposed that the council sell lots on the Marsh for five lives, later changed to 53 years. Rental would not be paid for the first two years, while the houses were being built. The lots were popular and were purchased, sometimes in bulk, by future mayors of the city as well as the serving sheriff, consolidating the view today that this was a corrupt city council feathering its own nest.[13] In his book *The Georgian Buildings of Bristol*, Walter Ison lists prominent Bristolians such as a Sheriff, James Hollidge, Stephen Peloquin, John Hobbs, John and Nathaniel Day and Woodes Rogers as early owners of property.[14]

On 23 October 1699, Dr John Reade made a petition to the council to build a house in the south side of the Marsh.[15] Reade believed that others wanted to build there too – and Ison has the mayor as one of these.[16] The lease was recorded three days later with building starting immediately – possibly creating, according to Dening, the 'first brick-fronted house erected within the City boundaries'.[17] Reade paid an annual rent of 40 shillings. This was not the first building on the Marsh. Some structures had been created in the seventeenth century. In 1628 there was a house and garden there, as well as a rope house.

Before any building could take place, the ground level of the Marsh had to be built up. A mix of industrial and domestic

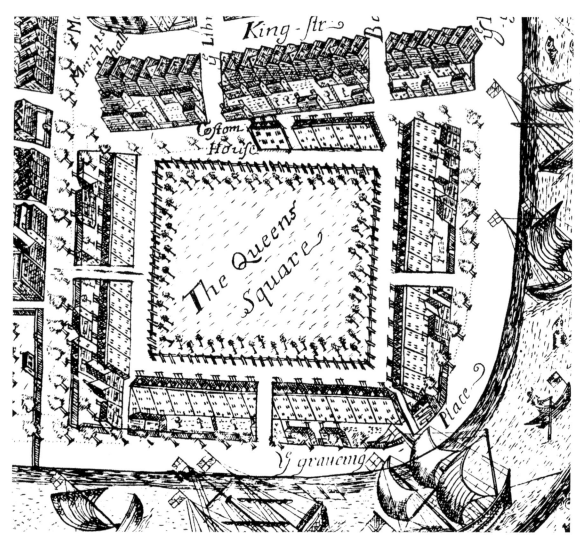

*The City of Bristoll*, 1710.
James Millerd.
[Bristol Museums & Art Gallery]

material was dumped quickly, raising the level by around two metres.

Unusually, the corporation took an active role in planning these developments right from the start. Everyone involved, it seemed, wanted a prestigious scheme. There was an attempt to create uniform frontages. In a major departure for Bristol, the corporation said houses should be built of brick and stone, with stone back and side walls, and a front made of brick with freestone quoins. A courtyard, with a brick wall, was to be placed in front. Development was quick. In February 1700 the bowling green was closed and attempts were made to buy the ropewalk.

There were problems in finding bricks. Mowl says that there was only one brick kiln in the city and complains that the city's most prestigious development to date had been passed to 'a workforce untrained in their medium . . . using bricks of inferior quality.'[18] Mowl believes this may have been due to Romsey owning a kiln – 'very Bristolian' – or, and this seems more likely, he had been inspired by seeing brick-built buildings during one of his many visits to London. Whatever, it was an architectural revolution for Bristol.

Twenty-five houses were built between 1700 and 1703 around three sides of the square. The south and west sides were popular, but no plots were leased on the back of King Street on the northern boundary. The square was not built in a unified way as, for example, John Wood had done in Queen Square in Bath, where, Ison says, 'the formal beauty of the architecture expressed the ideals and personality only of its architect-promoter.'[19] It was left to individual leaseholders to create the houses within the constraints laid down by the corporation as in early London developments.

However, there were some restrictions placed on use. Bristol Corporation would not allow commercial tenants, even though the dock was close by, nor workers' cottages. All noisy trades and those posing a fire hazard were banned. It was not an area for poor people to live, nor to work. From 1709, the corporation instructed leaseholders 'to build noe mean sordid building on any of the said Ground to be Receptacles for poor people etc nor to lett any house or building for shopps for Smiths, Workhouses for Chandlers, Publike Brewhouses, bakehouses or any other shoppes for Tradesmen'.[20] This did not stop some lofts and cellars being rented for use and in 1761 the Marine Coffee House and Tavern opened, though this was well after the square had been built and at a very different stage in its history. [21]

The area was still referred to as the Marsh in 1702. Given the elegant nature of the space being created, it was inevitable that a new name would follow. Queen Anne was visiting Bath in September that year. A deputation invited her to visit Bristol, which she did on 3 September 1702. A salute from the Marsh of 100 guns was followed by the Mayor and Aldermen agreeing 'that the Square now building in the Marsh shall be called "Queen Square"'. [22]

After the early development, there followed a period of boom and bust. No leases were issued between 1703 and 1708, though 25 were granted in 1709. By then, the square was nearly complete, with only the Custom House – finished in 1711, built at a cost of £2,525 and leased to the Crown for £120 annually – and the north-west corner left to build. The Custom House came to dominate the square, as can be seen in William Halfpenny's 'North Prospect of Queen Square'. Ison wrote:

> This Customs [sic] House was a three-story building of brick, with stone dressings and a wooden modillioned cornice, similar to the houses in the square but superior to them in dimensions and scale. From the ground-story there projected an Ionic colonnade of seven bays, the three middle ones being wider than those on either side. The brick face of the two-storied upper part was decorated with stone quoins, used like pilasters to form one wide

*Ye North Prospect of Queen Square in ye City of Briftol*, 1732. William Halfpenny.
[Bristol Museums & Art Gallery]

bay between two narrow ones, the former three windows wide and the latter two. The windows were spaced to centre over the bays of the colonnade; the usual intermediate stringcourse was omitted, and the middle window of the upper tier was replaced by superimposed panels of stone, one carved with the Royal Arms and the other a sundial.[23]

Work also started on the central space, which was laid out as a formal garden with gravel paths. Wooden railings were placed around the whole of the grassed area. Between 1704 and 1706 the roadway around the square was paved, and two rows of trees were planted in 1705 (a task for which George Adams, keeper of the square, was paid £27). In 1709, the Mansion House was built. Ropewalks were removed the next year after protests from tenants, the tar houses serving the roperies were pulled down, and more trees were planted in 1711. The central part of the square had more railings placed around it, with two lines of lime trees inside, and cross paths made of gravel were laid. By now most sides of the square had buildings on them and the following year proposals for the north-west corner were submitted. John Macky, a visitor to Bristol during this time, called it 'a very noble square, as

*Custom House*, 1820. Hugh O'Neill.
[Bristol Museums & Art Gallery]

Detail from Halfpenny's 1732 engraving showing full height railings in front of the Mansion House. [Bristol Museums & Art Gallery]

large as that of Soho in London: In which is kept the Custom-House; and most of the eminent Merchants, who keep their Coaches reside here.' [24]

Some local people liked it too. Writing in 1712, the master of Bristol Grammar School, William Goldwin, wrote 'A Poetical Description of Bristol' – a piece of doggerel but at least a heartfelt one. Goldwin described Queen Square as a creation arising from 'heaps of Rubbish':

.. What can't Inventress Art and Labour do?

This handsome Square from heaps of Rubbish grew;

And tho' past Years the marshy Bottom saw

Thick drizling Fogs from steaming Nature draw,

No vap'rish Humours left, but only those

Which Ladies sickly Fancies discompose:

Where level-walks delightful Lanes display,

There wat'ry Mud in deep Confusion lay.

So, when Appelles drew his master frame,

From jumbled Paint the pretty Venus came.

So Holland's Province built on boggy Lands

Consummate Neatness, and a Beauty stands:

Thus (since the Objects Similes provoke)

The whole Creation from a Chaos broke . . .

Halfpenny's engraving of 1732 shows the square as complete, though it was probably finished in 1728. Buck's *Bristol Prospect* shows the square filled with small trees in 1734. All of the houses were three storeys high, with roof garrets. If the house was single-fronted, it had three windows on each storey; if double-fronted, it had five. They were made of red brick dressed with freestone. Hoods sheltered most doorways, though some of the larger houses had shallow

Detail from Halfpenny's 1732 engraving showing east side of the square. [Bristol Museums & Art Gallery]

porches. There are two detailed examples: the first, No. 35, built for Woodes Rogers, seaman; the second, No. 29, built for Nathaniel Day between 1709 and 1711.

Woodes Rogers was a friend of Alexander Selkirk, the inspiration for Daniel Defoe's Robinson Crusoe. The plaque on No. 35 reads: 'Great Seaman, Circumnavigator, Colonial Governor.' Rogers did live there, but the plaque, like the claim about Selkirk, tells only half a story. Rogers did save Selkirk in February 1709 when his ship found him marooned. He was captain of a 'private ship of war'. The privateers were little more than government-sponsored pirates, paid to foment havoc among the enemies of Great Britain (other privateers included Sir Walter Raleigh and Sir Francis Drake). This they did, especially on the return trip, when enough ship's booty was taken to guarantee a huge profit for investors. Woodes Rogers was the most famous privateer of them all, as well as being a merchant with interests in the slave trade. His book, *A Cruising Voyage Around the World*, published in 1712, told the story of his trip. After encountering financial problems, he became governor of the Bahamas. He died in 1732, a possible victim of poisoning. The plaque puts a gloss on a less than reputable history.

The legend of Selkirk also needs unpicking. Defoe never met him and he may have been equally, if not more, inspired by the Duke's pilot, William Dampier (on the sister ship to Rogers'), who had written a book about his life which was in Defoe's private library. Selkirk did come to Bristol where he fought with a shipwright and is found by

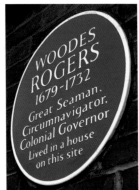

The Rogers' plaque on No. 35. [Stephen Morris]

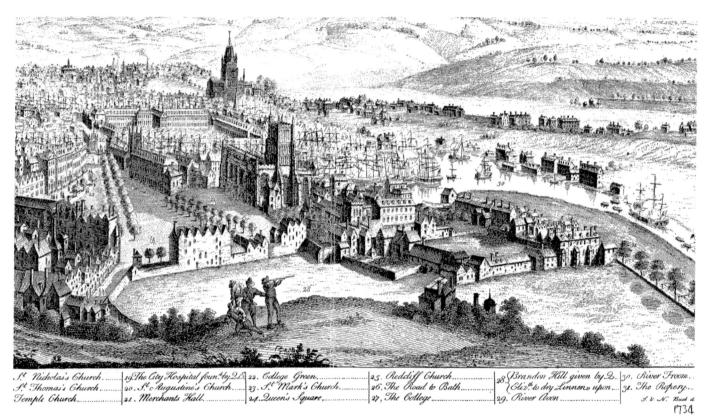

| | | | | |
|---|---|---|---|---|
| St. Nicholas's Church. | 19. The City Hospital foun.d by 2.E. | 22. College Green. | 25. Reddiff Church. | 28. Brandon Hill given by Q. | 30. River Froom. |
| St. Thomas's Church. | 20. St Augustine's Church. | 23. St Mark's Church. | 26. The Road to Bath. | Eliz.th to dry Linnen upon. | 31. The Ropery. |
| Temple Church. | 21. Merchants Hall. | 24. Queen's Square. | 27. The College. | 29. River Avon. | S & N. Buck d |
| | | | | | 1734 |

**North West Prospect of Bristol**, 1734. Buck. [BRL 27235 Or 31812]

biographers to be cruel to his wife, a bigamist, and a bully. [25]

Rogers had been given a 52-year lease in December 1702, paying a peppercorn rent for the first two years then 42 shillings annually (one shilling for each square foot of frontage). His was the first lease to record the name Queen Square. He agreed to build a 'substantial mansion'. The front of his house measured 42 feet, with a depth of 118 feet. There was a forecourt there, 10 feet deep, enclosed by a brick wall. The tops of walls were to be finished with wooden modillioned eaves-cornice. All other walls were made of stone. The lease said also that the timber and iron that were used were to be 'substantial'. Internally, the first storey was to be 11 feet high, the second 10 feet and the third, nine feet.

Rogers' house is no longer with us. Much of No. 29 – which Ison calls the most remarkable of them all – remains. Ison provides a detailed description:

> The front of this house is built of red brick laid in the customary Flemish bond, and tied in with its neighbours by nine-inch stone quoins with chamfered arrises, laid in long and short courses alternately. The ground-story contains a centrally-placed doorway, which has been altered, and two windows on either side, the fenestral

No. 29 Queen Square.
[National Monuments Record, Batsford C39/ 287)21]

pattern of the two upper stories being similar. The exposed sash-boxes are faced with architrave-mouldings and set almost flush with the building face, in window openings that have flat arches of gauged brickwork with stone keys carved into a variety of grotesque masks. The wooden modillioned eaves-cornice is almost identical with other examples in the square.

He added:

[This] description might be applied to many houses built about this time, but here the builder has chosen to add, in a rather illiterate fashion, ornaments drawn from the Classical repertory. Stone pediments, arranged in the usual sequence of the segmental form alternating with the triangular, are placed above the ground- and first-floor window arches, and engaged columns of the Roman Doric, Ionic and Corinthian orders, superimposed in that relation to the three stories, are used to divide the front into three bays, one narrow between two wide. The pedestals are omitted, and while the Doric and Ionic columns are given their appropriate entablatures, the Corinthian has only its architrave. Scrolled trusses take the place of the Doric entablatures on either side of the

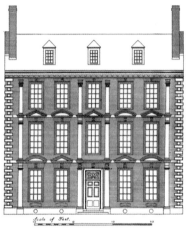

Elevation, No. 29.

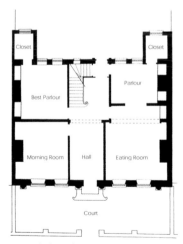

Ground plan of No. 29.

doorway, and support a flat stone hood which has a pan-
elled soffit. The forecourt was enclosed by fine railings
and an elaborate gate set between richly carved stone
piers... [26]

Mowl does not like it, calling it 'an elevation with all the
charm of untutored enthusiasm, a memory perhaps of the first
pages of a pattern book or some Oxford college gateway of
the 1630s. In no way is it urban design for the 18th century.'[27]

Whatever the recent reappraisals, it was clear that a remarkable square had been created. What was missing was a
centrepiece.

## Michael Rysbrack's William III ■

RIGHT IN THE CENTRE of the square is the equestrian statue of King William III, noble and triumphant, portraying the Roman Emperor conquering all. In *Sculpture in Bristol*, Douglas Merritt calls William III 'Bristol's most prestigious public statue'.[28] He is right but we should extend the praise: William III is the best equestrian statue by any sculptor in the eighteenth century, and possibly ever since, though revered elsewhere more than in Bristol. As Rysbrack's biographer said, it is 'too little known, for it may claim to be easily the best statue in England. If it were in a provincial town on the continent sightseers would go a long way to see this.'[29]

Rysbrack's masterwork has been moved three times, and although it has always occupied the centre area of the square, it has not always faced exactly the same direction. It was moved first in the late 1930s when the inner circuit road was built and it was placed on an island in the middle of the dual carriageway facing the city centre; next when it was sent to the Duke of Beaufort's home at Badminton Park during the Second World War (it was returned to the square in 1948); and finally when it was restored in 1999 to its original position, without the railings and with new lighting.

Work on the statue started in 1731, 29 years after the monarch's death. William of Orange, a Dutch prince, had ascended to the throne in 1688 after the Glorious Revolution. He had not been popular, especially amongst Catholics, indeed had been hated – William had replaced the Catholic James II – though many places fought to get statues of him erected. The Bristol Corporation, who commissioned the statue, wanted a central point in the square now that building work had finished. They were helped by John Elbridge, a local philanthropist.

The Bristol merchants and the Common Council led the fundraising effort in an attempt to emulate, or even beat, London where a similar statue was planned. Bristol Corporation paid £500 to Elbridge in August 1733, with £300 coming from the Merchant Venturers the following year. More was needed, though. They requested support from 'gentlemen and other inhabitants' to help create a monument to 'the memory of our Great and Glorious Deliverer the late King William III'.

Fundraising efforts seemed to have failed: nearly £710 still had to be found by the time the statue was in place and both the Corporation (finding another £500) and the Merchant Venturers (£200) made additional contributions.

Rysbrack competed for the commission against Peter Scheemakers, whose own statue of William ended up in Hull.

Rysbrack's William III. [Stephen Morris]

Trained in Antwerp, Rysbrack (1694-1770) had come to London in 1720 where he worked with James Gibbs, the architect. Possibly the leading designer and sculptor of eighteenth-century England, Rysbrack's work included tombs, busts and statues in Westminster Abbey, the Temple of British Worthies in Stowe and many other places. His first work in Bristol was a monument to Andrew Innys, past Master of the Merchant Venturers, in the church of St John the Baptist in 1726.

Rysbrack began work on his clay model in May 1733. A year later it had been cast by Van Oost, better known as a painter of flowers. It travelled to Bristol by boat in July 1735, though it was to be another 14 months before Bristol's mayor could announce that it had been erected and placed on its pedestal made of Portland stone (it is likely that this was made elsewhere too). Railings, with lamps, were placed around the statue, and gravel paths and landscaping implemented. Rysbrack was paid £1,800.[30] Scheemakers got £50.

The statue needed repairs in 1749. The town clerk wrote to Rysbrack to tell him that the defects 'are of such a kind as if not soon remedyed will absolutely ruin a Statue which well deserves to be as lasting as it is elegant and beautiful.' [31]

With the statue made from brass, not the usual bronze, and a work of great beauty, it is little wonder that William III is listed Grade I by English Heritage who describe it as 'an outstanding example' of the work of the artist. It proved to be a focus for civic pride in the renovation of the square in 2000. Around the statue is now carved: 'This inscription commemorates the return of this historic space to the citizens of Bristol. The work was completed in the year 2000 through the support of the Heritage Lottery Fund, Bristol City Council and the Queen Square Association.'

## The Square before the Riots

■

BRISTOL WAS STILL a major centre of trade in 1740 and, with a population of 50,000, it had overtaken Norwich to be the leading provincial city. The city specialised in shipbuilding, tobacco and sugar. Indeed, the port was especially useful for attracting trade in goods that needed processing, with glass-making, brewing, distilling and sugar-refining strong. Queen Square must have offered some respite from the busy, bustling city. Most Bristolians lived in poor conditions and are likely to have gazed with some envy upon the square and its inhabitants. Writing to a friend in 1739, Alexander Pope said: 'I hardly knew what I undertook when I said I would give you some account of this place. Nothing can do it but a picture, it is so unlike any scene you ever saw.' He added:

> You see twenty odd pyramids smoking over the town and a vast extent of houses red and white. You come first to old walls and over a bridge built on both sides like London Bridge, and was as much crowded, with a strong mixture of seamen, women, children, loaded horses, asses and sledges with goods dragging along. From thence you come to a key ...and in the middle of the street, as far as you can see, hundreds of ships, their masts as thick as they can stand by one another, which is the oddest and

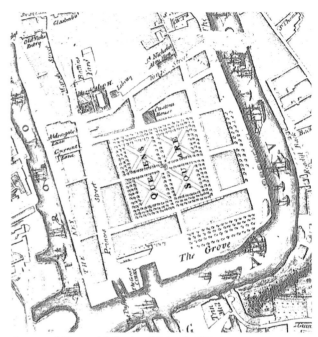

*Survey of City and Suburbs of Bristol*, 1750. Rocque.
[BRL B 29604]

> most surprising sight imaginable.

The square was one of the few things he liked about Bristol. He wrote: 'Nothing is fine in it but the square, which is larger than Grosvenor-Square and wellbuilded, with a very fine brass statue in the middle of K. William on Horseback; and the key which is full of shops and goes half round this

*Queen Square Bristol from North West Corner*, 1827. TL Rowbotham. [Bristol Museums & Art Gallery]

Square.'[32] As John Sansom wrote in *Bristol First* 'This was the Age of Reason . . . and it is easy to see why Pope preferred the order of Queen Square to the riot of Bristol's medieval streets.'[33]

In September 1761, the American architect resident in Bristol, James Bridges, who was influential in the design of St Nicholas Church among others, created a temporary building in the square. The Temple of Fireworks display, 73 feet high, was the centrepiece of the festivities held to celebrate the coronation of George III.

In 1764, the gravel paths were turfed over. Twelve years later, the whole square was redesigned, the ground and the walks re-laid, and a drain laid. The inner row of trees was removed. It was still liked. In one article in *Gentleman's Magazine* in 1789 an anonymous commentator wrote: 'The best-built parts of Bristol are the College-green, some of the streets in the neighbourhood, and Queen-Square.'[34] The barber-surgeon and antiquary, William Barrett, praised the square in 1789 in his *History and Antiquities of Bristol* 'for its delightful walks, shaded with rows of elms, and the cross walks with lime-trees, is esteemed an agreeable place of habitation, as well as of resort in fine weather, for the gentle-

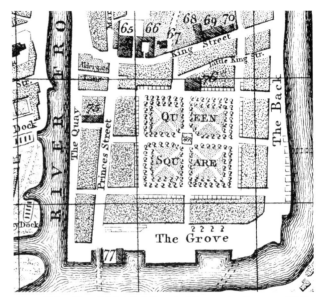

*Plan of the City of Bristol delineated from actual survey*, 1773. Benjamin Donne. [BRL B23549]

men and ladies'.[35] Seven years later the lime trees were removed as there was too much shade. The council maintained the square: maintenance of the cross walks cost £40 in 1786 for labour and gravel.

Who lived in the square? For much of the early part of its life it was the home of prominent businessmen. It was also a civic and political centre. The official residence of the mayor was the Mansion House in the north-east corner of the square,

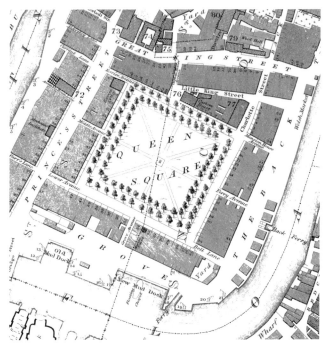

***Map of Bristol***, 1829. George C Ashmead.
[Bristol Museums & Art Gallery]

purchased in 1786, though the main council house was in Corn Street, about 10 minutes' walk away.

Many of the houses were occupied by those involved in the slave trade. By the 1730s, Bristol had become the country's main slaving port, overtaking London. It would remain so for 15 years, after which it was overtaken by Liverpool. Even as late as 1789, the trade between Africa and the West Indies comprised over 80 per cent of the total value of Bristol's overseas trade, though the trade in people was in decline and between 1803 and 1807, when the British slave trade ended, it had one per cent of the share. Nevertheless, between 1698 and 1807 there were 2,100 slaving voyages from Bristol with over half-a-million slaves carried from Africa to the American continent. Today it is hard to believe that this odious trade took place, let alone lasted so long.

An anonymous comment in *Bristol Past and Present* published in 1882 claimed that 'There is not a brick in the city but what is cemented with the blood of a slave.'[36] The most prominent residents in the square (10 out of 24 ratepayers according to Madge Dresser, author of *Slavery Obscured*) 'were connected in a dense web of business and kinship interests either to the African slave trade or, increasingly as the century wore on, to the trade in slave-produced commodities.'[37] Dresser identifies, among others, John Day, a leading merchant and representative for Bristol at the government's investigation into the trade between 1711 and 1713, and James Laroche, manager of around 132 slaving voyages. One of his shipments included 40 children.

Elias Vanderhorst, a slave owner and square resident, became the first American consul to Britain in 1792, having arrived in Bristol twenty years before. A plaque marks this piece of history. Another shows that Kosciuszko, the Polish patriot, was a guest of the consul in 1799, prior to going to America, having escaped imprisonment in Russia. Some of the square's residents who were involved in the slave trade were also prominent in the Bristol Corporation and in the city's burgeoning cultural life, such as the opening of the Theatre Royal (now known as the Bristol Old Vic) in nearby King Street in 1776.

Others to have lived in the square include, at No. 33, Eça de Quieroz, the Portuguese Dickens and his country's consul for 10 years from 1878. He wrote part of *Letters from England* while working there. David Hume, the philosopher, worked at No. 16, but was dismissed by his employer for criticising his use of English. Three doors along, at No. 19, Edmund Burke stayed during the election of 1774, when he became a Bristol MP.

By the beginning of the nineteenth century, the square began to lose some of its grandeur. With the increasingly commercial nature of the nearby area, the conversion of back

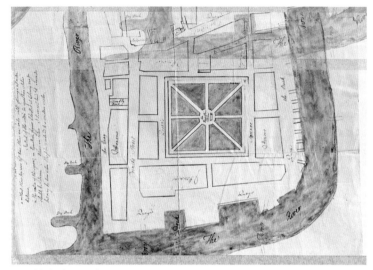

Unpublished map of Queen Square – possibly the one presented by J Plumley, in 1814. [BRL B 28842]

premises into large warehouses, and the smell from sewage trapped in the Floating Harbour, the square was no longer the desirable property it once had been. Country houses became more popular than city ones among the wealthier merchants, as did the area of Clifton and parts of Bath. Bristol was in gentle decline: the docks were beginning to suffer from the increase in size of ships (the harbour could not take them and they found it difficult to navigate the Avon), trade was suffering, and the moral outrage against the slave trade was begin-

*22 Queen Square*, 1820.
Hugh O'Neill. [Bristol
Museums & Art Gallery]

ning to bite. The corporation and the merchants, traditionally
conservative groups, failed to anticipate the need for change.
Some modernisation of the square did take place – in 1819
gas lamps were introduced – but it was not enough. For all
these reasons, and most of all the Bristol riots of 1831, the
square as the home for the élite of Bristol society was coming
to an end.

## The Bristol Riots, 1831 ■

QUEEN SQUARE has provided a place for assembly and protest, especially that targeted at local and national government, owing to its housing the mayor and the customs offices. The corporation procession took place every year in the square, and polling booths were erected there. Thousands of placards were placed there during elections. Queen Square, like other open spaces in the city, allowed easy access to demonstrators denied use of other properties and land.

Queen Square has a violent past, dating back to the Marsh: in 1549 and 1561 there were 'riotous assemblies', the first in opposition to the mayor, the second leading to the removal of the gates.[38] Thomas Beddoes, a radical and scientist, called in 1788 for William III to be 'draped in black mourning til our liberties be secure'[39] and in 1795 asked the people to rally against Prime Minister Pitt's legislation opposing radicalism. A bloody loaf and note attacking corruption was attached to a railing in 1800.

It was not the only area of the city where riots took place. There was Jacobite rioting in 1714 which had led to the passing of the Riot Act. There was trouble again in 1783 when seamen protested about the Society of Merchant Venturers, in 1791 with the Church and King riot, and in 1795 when troops attacked a mob near Bristol Bridge. The statue of George III in Portland Square was destroyed in 1813 during a reform rally.[40] The corporation was the focus of protest in the late eighteenth and early nineteenth centuries, and there was a large gathering against Catholic emancipation in 1829. Elections and drunken attacks on losing candidates seemed to go hand in hand for a time.[41]

But it was the three-day rioting of 1831 in Queen Square that is mostly remembered today. Twelve people are known to have died, others were too burnt to allow identification, and five more were hanged, with 77 either imprisoned or deported.[42] Many private houses on two sides of the square were destroyed – the north side completely, and most houses on the west – as were key civic buildings, including the Custom House, Mansion House, the Excise Office, the city jails, six warehouses and the Bishop's Palace.[43] In all, 29 houses were destroyed in the square. After the riots, two cartloads of broken glass were taken away so that horses would not be injured.

The writer, Charles Kingsley, remembered standing on St Michael's Hill in north Bristol as a 12-year-old looking down onto the city which was then 'a bright mass of flame, almost

*Queen Square on the Night of October 30th*, 1831. JB Pyne. [BRL Portfolio 2 B 23076)]

like a half-risen sun.' He said: 'The flames increased, multiplied at one point after another; till by ten o'clock that night one seemed to be looking down upon Dante's Inferno'. He heard

the multitudinous moan and wail of lost spirits surging to and fro amid that sea of fire ... dull explosions down below mingled with the roar of the mob, and the infernal hiss and crackle of the flames.

He could see for many miles, too:

I could see the lovely tower of Dundry shining red – the symbol of the old faith, looking down in stately wonder and sorrow upon the fearful birth-throes of a new age.[44]

What had caused this remarkable outbreak of violence? One issue of national significance was political reform. At this time, few could vote – between 25 and 33 per cent of adult males in the city were eligible. In addition, parliamentary constituencies were spread unevenly: Bristol had two MPs for example, while Manchester and Bradford, like some other large cities, had none. Calls for more democracy had been ignored by the Tory-controlled Commons and met often with repression – the massacre at Peterloo had taken place only 12 years before, when at least 12 people were murdered as troops attacked a reform rally.

The Reform Bill had been approved by Parliament by one vote in November 1830, but had been defeated in committee. This would have removed some of the rotten boroughs and enfranchised the rapidly developing cities. Parliament was dissolved in April 1831 and Earl Grey, the Prime Minister, called an immediate election, which the pro-reform Whigs won. Bristol elected two Whig MPs, though only one was a reformer. The Reform Bill was passed in September, only to be defeated in the Tory-dominated Lords. King William IV refused to create more Whig peers, Grey resigned, and the Duke of Wellington was asked to form a government. Some Tories, realising that reform was popular, refused to serve. One of them, Robert Peel, feared that civil war might result from Wellington's government.

The position was chaotic. King William, now unpopular, asked Grey to become Prime Minister again, and agreed to create the peers he wanted. The Lords passed the Reform Act. Whether it was all worth it was another matter. The franchise failed to embrace working people, given the property require-ment, and women were still barred. The reform of the constit-uencies also failed to remove iniquities: 35 had MPs elected by no more than 300 registered voters.

Charles Pinney.

Reform was unquestionably popular in Bristol, even though it was clear that few would benefit from it, and Bristol was unaffected by the proposed changes to seats in the House of Commons. There was a literate workforce who could read political notices, and debate was strong: five newspapers covered all political interests. In the summer of 1831, one petition in favour of reform (there were at least four that year) had been collected with 17,000 signatures – nearly three times as many as those that voted in the 1832 election. A counter-reform petition, organised by the Tory White Lion Club, who feared that limited reform would lead to universal suffrage, was signed by 5,000 Bristolians, though the majority of these were likely to have been from outside the city.[45]

At least two peaceful rallies were held in the square in mid-October (other cities, such as Nottingham, Derby and London had seen riots). Bristol's mayor, Charles Pinney, in office for less than two months when the riots broke out, was personally a supporter of reform (and possibly of slavery – he was linked to the trade), though his party was not. Bristol was not to get a pro-reform mayor for another 21 years.

Even though the crowd called for 'The King and reform' there were other reasons for the Bristol riots – principally local political corruption. It is noticeable that in other cities where the reform movement was strong, riots happened soon after the bill's collapse, while in Bristol three weeks passed without a reaction. There had been no riots at any pro-reform gatherings. Planning for the riots seemed non-existent, there were no leaders (though many were tried as such afterwards) and no weapons had been stockpiled, the rioters using literally whatever came to hand. However, neither was it just hooligans: 'the polite way in which residents were ordered to leave, the decoration of William III's statue with a cap of liberty, the introduction of circle dancing on the grass and the systematic liberation of the city's four gaols, suggest a degree of organization', according to Steve Poole.[46]

For Susan Thomas 'it was the fate of the city Corporation, and not that of the Reform Bill, which was really at issue in Bristol in 1831'.[47] She said the rioters:

made it clear to the whole city that the Corporation's

claim to represent the people of Bristol would be judged on its ability to handle the visit of the unpopular Recorder. The refusal of the 'respectable' classes to help control the riot was thus an emphatic rejection of a city government which had become totally alienated from its subjects, having ruled for decades without either consulting or considering them.[48]

Bristol's arrogant, secretive corporation, with its restricted membership, poor public services and high taxes, was resented. The formation of the Bristol Chamber of Commerce in 1823 did not help, as it was made up of similarly corrupt interests, though they did campaign strongly for reduced dues (by 1848 Bristol was the most costly port in the country).[49] The riots were therefore an attack on the government of the city, wrapped up in the campaign for reform.

One can point also to the incompetence of the military in failing to keep and, once the riots had started, restore order. The refusal of Bristol's middle-class citizens to police the city was another reason: many of them were supporters of reform and members of the Bristol Political Union – one of many pro-reform groups in the country. Pinney could not stop the violence through establishing a citizens' posse as those he asked

to join objected to his failure to support the reform movement once in office. Even when the churches asked them to help, they continued to refuse.

Whatever the causes, the order of events is clear. Sir Charles Wetherell, Recorder of Bristol (for which he got a hogshead of sherry and 100 guineas), resident of London, MP for Boroughbridge in Yorkshire, ex-Attorney General – but still a senior enforcer of the law – came to the city on 29 October to open the

Sir Charles Wetherell.

assizes at the Guildhall. He had told the House that Bristolians were 'indifferent to reform'.[50] Wetherell had a selfish motivation: he would lose his seat if the reform bill became law. At this time, Boroughbridge had two MPs elected by fewer than 50 people. Little wonder that Wetherell was called 'the *primo buffo* of the anti-reformers' by *Carpenter's Monthly Political Magazine*.[51]

Wetherell, accompanied by Bristol MP Edward Protheroe jr, a reformer who believed that protestors would be peaceful, was met at Totterdown by large crowds. Ironically, he had been fêted two years before when he had opposed Catholic emancipation – he had resigned his post as Attorney General in Wellington's government – possibly by some of those who opposed him now. He managed to open the assizes and went to have dinner with the mayor at the Mansion House. Facing crowds of almost 3,000 people who refused to leave the square, the mayor was forced to read the Riot Act. Members of the crowd pulled up railings as weapons and were about to set fire to the Mansion House when troops arrived. Wetherell meanwhile, in disguise, or at least without the clothes by which he could be recognised, scuttled to safety over the roofs and left Bristol the next day. Posters were printed announcing that he had left.

The Mansion House was attacked on the 30th with no troops available – or prepared – to defend it. Protestors, drunk on the ransacked wines and spirits (the mayor had a well-stocked cellar) next turned their attack to houses on the north side of the square. The Custom House was looted and burned – charred timbers in the basement can still be seen today. The following morning, *Felix Farley's Bristol Journal*, a conservative newspaper, said:

Monday morning presented such a spectacle as has never been witnessed in this place. The appearance of Queen Square was appalling in the extreme, most of the houses were but heaps of ruins, others were still flaming with vehemence, whilst every now and then walls fell with a tremendous crash around; in various parts lay several of the rioters, in the last stages of senseless intoxication, and with countenances more resembling fiends than men.[52]

In the Bishop's Palace, a relative of the Bishop wrote on 30 October to the Home Secretary: 'The City of Bristol is at present entirely in the possession of an organised *Banditti*, of the very vilest and yet of a most dastardly description.'[53] The Bishop's Palace was burnt down that day. Both the Bishop of Bristol and the Bishop of Bath and Wells (who had been greeted with stones and mud when in Bristol on 24 October) had voted with the majority in the House of Lords against reform.

By Monday morning it was clear that it was not just the square that would be damaged. Major Digby Mackworth, a member of the Horse Guards, found two sides of the square burning. As the protestors tried to enter a house adjacent to the ships in the harbour, he feared that not only would the

*North Side of Queen Square Bristol the morning after the Dreadful Conflagration*, 1831. JB Pyne. [BRL Portfolio 2B23051]

*West Side of Queen Square Bristol the morning after the Dreadful Conflagration*, 1831 JB Pyne. [BRL Portfolio 2 B 23052]

ships themselves be burned, but the whole of Bristol would be affected. He gave the order to charge. His actions stopped the protest, even though this resulted in deaths.

The military operation generally had been a shambles. Magistrates refused to lead the troops against the crowds, as they had in 1793 in another riot at the Toll-bridge where 11 people had been killed. Apart from the fact that they said they could not ride, 'They were afraid to make a public

appearance in case it increased their unpopularity and incited the mob to destroy their own shipping and warehouses in the city centre'.[54] With fewer than 100 regular constables in the city, special constables had to be brought in. Few merchants and tradespeople provided support. Instead hired thugs, resented by the demonstrators and condemned as 'hireling Tory-bludgeon men' by the *Bristol Mercury*, were recruited. Some of the troops – especially those known as the Bloody Blues who had suppressed riots in the West Country previously – were resented as well, though local forces, based in Bristol, were treated with more sympathy. No central co-ordination point had been agreed and there was confusion about lines of command. The mayor and the troops' leader, Brereton, a long-term resident in the city and sympathetic to reform, did not trust each other, and there was nervousness about an attack given the deaths at the Toll-bridge and Peterloo: in fact, Brereton refused to give the order to open fire and withdrew his troops for a time. Little wonder it took three days to regain order.

One man caught up in the riots was Isambard Kingdom Brunel, in Bristol to work on his new bridge over the Avon Gorge, the project which was to become the Clifton Suspension Bridge, one of the engineering wonders of the nineteenth century. The riots were one of the many reasons why the bridge was not finished until 1864, five years after Brunel's death. He had arrived the day after the riot had started. As the rioting worsened, he was sworn in as a special constable, and actually arrested one man who was later taken away by another constable who was, it turned out, a fellow rioter in disguise. He wrote in his diary:

> Having dressed went down to Bristol heard that there had been some fires and that the 14th were gone – could hardly believe it – went to the Mansion House – found it nearly deserted – it had been broken into again and sacked – armed myself with a chair back and found the guard – Admiral Hillhouse and Mr Roache [Brunel's friends] busy getting the pictures and plate by the roof and through the custom house.[55]

Brunel gave evidence later at the trial of Pinney, though he was not able to identify any rioters.[56]

Isambard Kingdom Brunel.
[Public Record Office, London]

## Queen Square after the Riots ■

IT WAS TO TAKE MANY YEARS for a normal life to return to the square. There was the issue of responsibility and blame for a start, and the need to restore normality to the area. Wetherell wanted to be in charge of legal proceedings but the government appointed a commission. Over 100 men were tried: 26 were condemned to death and 55 others were convicted. Pinney was found not guilty of neglect of duty and Brereton committed suicide during his trial. A petition signed by 10,000 Bristolians appealed for the death sentences to be commuted. Five of the 26 were hanged. The rest, along with seven convicted men, were sent to Botany Bay. All others convicted suffered hard labour.[57]

There seemed little change to politics. Reform of the political system had been tepid and Conservatives were still elected to serve Bristol nationally and locally, though they held on in the city only by sleight-of-hand.[58] The elections were held in the square, and the placing of polling booths near the ruins is thought to have helped the Conservatives win (in addition to their usual well-organised campaign).[59] Queen Square was otherwise avoided, especially when it was proposed that a dinner be held there to mark the assent of the Reform Bill.

The *Bristol Mercury* supported the proposal:

We are aware that, as a body, the reformers have been branded as the authors of the mischief which the ruins of the square bear witness to; but we would not, on that account, advise them to forego the use of it on the present occasion, if it should appear to be their interest to assemble there, and thus show how utterly they hold the calumny in contempt.[60]

Another indication that little had changed politically was that Wetherell remained Recorder until 1846 when he died in a carriage accident.

Financial disputes meant that it was some time before the square could be rebuilt, though Henry Rumley built, on the north and west side, a series of Grecian terrace-houses in 1833. At first, owners wanted to see their leases released to the Bristol corporation. The corporation, however, did not want to bear the costs of repair and rebuilding and, after pressure, leaseholders took over the task, submitting bills for compensation, mostly when work was finished. Repairs to some houses did not start until mid-1833, and the square's centre – the place for relaxation and leisure – was still unkempt in 1837.

Residents asked the corporation for help that year so that

**North Side of Queen Square**, 1832. Rev. Eden (attrib). [Bristol Museums & Art Gallery]

the square could 'as it formerly did, afford a most desirable place of recreation and exercise, not only to its inhabitants but to those residing in the neighbourhood'.[61] Once finished, professional-class people occupied some of the houses – the 1841 census has merchants and accountants, among others. Now, though, some houses were turned into dwellings for multiple occupation, and lodging houses began to appear. It was also attracting undesirable attention. 'Queen Square appears to be entirely given up to the abuse of the very scum of society', *Felix Farley's Bristol Journal* said in June 1837:

> gangs of boys and men are allowed to dig up the grass plots, play at pitch and toss, climb the trees for the bird's nests, hurling stones and using the most filthy language and gestures with impunity.[62]

At the election a month later, fighting broke out again in the square. Though this was not as serious as in 1831, it damaged further the reputation of the square, summed up by the *Bristol Mirror* as 'neglected and miserable'. The removal of the wooden railings in the fighting let in 'fowls and vagabonds', and horses and carts were allowed to drive in and cut up the grass. To protect the square in future, iron railings were erected at the perimeter.

*Lavar's Panorama of Bristol*, 1887. [Bristol Museums & Art Gallery]

The residents that were left, and no doubt the corporation and the police, must have been worried later that year when the Bristol Branch of the Working Men's Association held their first Chartist demonstration in October in the square. The handbill called on the 'Working Men of Bristol!' to 'arouse from your apathy, – learn your just rights, and how to maintain them!' The demonstration was peaceful, and future

Summer in the square, *c.*1850. [Reece Winstone Archive]
Below, sheep grazing in the square in February 1895. The park ranger's wooden hut can be seen behind the railings.
[Reece Winstone Archive]

assemblies took place nearby on Brandon Hill or in the Guildhall. The Chartist movement was not strong in Bristol, surprisingly, given the support for political reform.[63]

By the 1861 census, few professionals now lived in the square. Most houses were used by lodgers. There was little change by 1881: many of the buildings were offices or business houses, the rest being houses in multiple occupation. The Italian consul lived at No. 31. Some were occupied by actors and comedians working in the Theatre Royal nearby. By 1891 the square was mainly home to dock workers rather than professionals.

# Queen Square in the Twentieth Century ■

THE SQUARE FACED many new problems in the twentieth century, before it was renewed in the last decade. The square was now a place for work. In 1923, Dening wrote: 'Queen Square is now entirely given over to commercial purposes. A number of houses have been demolished, and others are so mutilated internally that scarcely anything of value remains.'[64] He compared it unfavourably with Queen Square Bath. This was still a residential area, though this was also given over to offices in time. Writing in 1952, Walter Ison shared Dening's view, and went on to claim that while the riots may have destroyed some of the properties, the 'inroads of commercial-

ism have had far more serious effects, for fine houses were destroyed to make way for hybrid monstrosities, while others have been mutilated.'[65]

A handful of houses were still lived in during the twentieth century, and there is one family house occupied in 2002. Twelve to 15 different families lived there in the 1930s, though most of these were probably caretakers. Mothers often used the benches to sit and watch their children play. There was even a jobsworth keeper, the park ranger, who had a hut near the Custom House. Others who lived there remember sheep grazing and school physical education lessons on the grass.

*16 Queen Square*, c 1910. S Loxton. [BRL]

1936, with statue of King William III and 'twig' metal seats. [Reece Winstone Archive]

Some recall fears of William III – "King Billy" – the square bogeyman who, they said, rode round the square at night to frighten the children.

Frank Ward remembers races round the square, and bonfires where office rubbish could be disposed. Clifford Richards and his family lived in 54 Queen Square until 1948, one of only a handful of residential houses remaining (they included No. 30 and No. 31). He remembers it as being very pleasant, with children playing in the square and adults strolling in the summer. Irene Ashton, born in the square at No. 50, recalls the beautifully ornate ceiling in her front room, the flights of stairs (they lived above some offices) and has never forgotten the ones she climbed daily: 13, seven, 11, nine. 'At the top of the house', she said, 'we would climb out of a small window on to a small balcony and watch the cannons being fired on Brandon Hill at 11.00am on Armistice Day.'[66] She remembers too the hot-cross-bun boy on Good Friday, the milkman and his horse and cart, and the man with a large pole who would light the gaslights outside the house.

Lawrence Brightman worked at No. 1 between 1935 and 1938 as assistant to the Vice-Consul for Portugal and Colombia, John Albano Fraser. Brightman used to raise the Portug-uese flag. He ended his work there when Fraser, a supporter of General Franco (his books *Franco Means Business* and *This Spanish Democracy* were published by a local press in Lewins Mead), passed the role to someone else. Fraser was also the author of *Spain and the West Country* and was branch secretary of the National Union of Seamen. Brightman loved the square, and recalls fondly how business people would park their cars under the supervision of members of the Corps of Commissionaires, a group of Great War veterans.

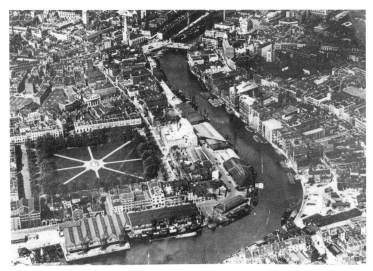

Aerial view of Queen Square before the introduction of Redcliffe Way [BRO 37167/ 151]

Clifford Richards remembers the road being driven through the square in 1937. The problems the square faced in the twentieth century were mainly due to the motor car. Though not as exciting a topic as political reform, traffic proved to be just as destructive for the square as the riots had been. In 1914 it was proposed that a bridge be built across the Floating Harbour with a feeder road down the south side of the square. In the 1920s a similar scheme was put forward. Both failed at the planning stage. In 1936 the decision was taken to build a 60ft road diagonally across the square. Designed by Sir George Oatley, the respected Bristol architect who had built the Wills Memorial Tower, work began on Redcliffe Way quickly, providing work for the unemployed. Trees were felled, and some houses on the north-west and south-east corners demolished. Rysbrack's statue, no longer regarded as a beautiful sculpture, was temporarily relocated to London. On its return, it was placed on an island in the middle of the road itself, with new planting and architectural features surrounding it, though these were nothing more than steps and seats.

The result was the end of the square as a space for relaxation and heritage. Even though the railings around the square had been removed in the 1920s to allow room for games, heavy traffic from the 1930s onwards would have made the area less of the playground it had become known for. Horrible though it was, the scheme was implemented easily – the opposition from the Queen Square Protest Committee was limited and harmed, perhaps, by their proposal that the road should go around the square. It was a *fait accompli*, too, with contractors securing the site early one morning and starting their work before the opposition could be aroused. Destruction on this scale would not happen now, even if the tactics used by the contractors are depressingly familiar. Local authorities are generally more enlightened and amenity societies far stronger and more influential than seventy years ago.

The scheme also seemed to take in that great lover of Bristol, John Betjeman. In his BBC talk of 12 April 1937, he said:

Bristol has not such a difficult traffic problem as London. What problem there is will be partially solved by the four ring roads which I am told are being built round the city. One of them, the inner one, runs right across Queen Square. This is unfortunate, but unavoidable. If we have many motor cars, we must pay the price not only in tax and the cost of the car but also in the scenery which motors are intended to take us to see. The road through Queen Square is part of a circle round the inner part of Bristol, which, it is intended, will divert that most unpleasant rush of traffic on to Bristol Bridge.[67]

By 1964, Betjeman had changed his views. In 'The Ideal Town' he wrote:

> What better place to start a townscape walk in England than the City of London – although York, Norwich, Bristol and even parts of Exeter may provide less mutilated examples? It will have to be on a Sunday because cars are the enemies of a civilised city, and we are still too barbarous to realise they must be kept without the walls.[68]

Little was to change in Queen Square for fifty years, despite efforts being made to protect the architectural integrity of the square, or that which was left. Even the Second World War seemed to pass the square by, except for the air raid shelters placed there (one, built in 1938, was found in the archaeological excavation in 1998). The Luftwaffe had targeted the city and large parts of central Bristol were destroyed. Half a block of half-timbered houses in King Street, and parts of the quadrangle of the Merchant Venturers' Almshouses, were damaged;

Aerial view of Queen Square after the introduction of Redcliffe Way. [BRO 37167/ 151]

the adjoining Merchant Venturers' Hall itself was destroyed. Nearby, the docks were hit heavily as was the Redcliffe area, but St Mary Redcliffe – the church Queen Elizabeth I praised on her visit to the Marsh 366 years before – was saved. As for the square, it escaped surprisingly unscathed, though there was some limited damage caused by incendiary devices.

Since 1950, Queen Square has featured in most major plans put forward for the city centre by either Bristol City Council or Avon County Council. By now, fewer than one-third

Nos. 36-42 Queen Square, with railings, 1941.
[National Monuments Record]

Open frontage, 31 Queen Square in 1942. [National Monuments Record]

Nos. 3-9 Queen Square, showing railings and forecourt walls, 1950. [National Monuments Record]

of the original houses were left. In 1952 Bristol, still suffering war damage, published its first-ever development plan. The plan described Queen Square as 'Public Open Space', with the perimeter being a 'Principal Car Park' (many cars – and even some horse-drawn carts – were using the area in 1951). The buildings were dedicated primarily for business use, offices and wholesale warehouses. Twenty-eight units in the Queen Square area were recorded as residential units, but it is not known how many of these were in the square itself.

The area was seen as architecturally important in the plan, development was restricted, and most of the buildings in the square were listed as Grade II, with the Custom House at Grade II* and the William III statue at Grade I. Twelve years later, the council made the whole central area, which included Queen Square, an Area of Special Control so that its unique character could be protected.

By the mid-1960s the square was facing further pressure. Increased traffic in the city resulting from economic growth, larger levels of employment in the central area and the new M4 and M5 motorways were affecting it badly. Already some boundary walls had been removed to allow forecourt parking. Controlled parking in 1964 through parking meters in the square and new multi-storey parking created elsewhere in the city, helped restrict excessive on-street parking, though this solution proved to be not so clever in the long term. The council wanted Redcliffe Way closed, but only if circumstances allowed. Despite all this, and piecemeal development, the square still, according to the city council, retained 'a fine overall scale and appearance.'[69]

A major step forward was the creation of the Queen Square Conservation Area in 1972, introduced under the 1967

Roundabout on Redcliffe Way at junction of Prince Street and King Street, 1951. [BRO 37167/ 16]

The Custom House before 1950. [National Monuments Record]

Queues of traffic in the square in 1970.
[Bristol City Council]

Queen Square prior to road closure.

Civic Amenities Act. For the first time, the council had a duty to take into account whether developments would enhance or preserve the conservation area. They wanted existing forecourt parking ended and no new forecourt parking allowed. The Historic Buildings Council for England recognized the importance of the square and started restoration by giving grant aid to No. 29.

By 1976 Queen Square was once again an address of prestige, though this time for offices, mostly involved in services. In 1977 the council looked at the decline of the docks and called again for the removal of Redcliffe Way. In the meantime, it suggested that only buses should be allowed to use the square, though this was not implemented immediately. Nor did the fact that the council owned three sides of the square prove to be much use. Although forecourt parking could be restricted fully, little was done to enforce the restriction for most properties. The council did call for the original railings to be re-introduced.

The restoration of some of the south side was undertaken by encouraging office development which finally brought to an end a century and a half of decline and vacancy in the square. That was the last major change to the square for 13 years, apart from the reinstatement of 12 forecourts. Despite the fact that the majority of those allowing parking on their forecourts had neither planning permission, nor proof of long-term use, the council was reluctant to take action to enforce their planning policy. Few tenants, it was felt, would give up such privileges unless they were offered new parking close by.

There was growing support for change, though. The council was supported by The Georgian Group and many other amenity societies. The council did say that they intended to restore the square to its former appearance consistent with its Conservation Area status. This was favoured by most tenants of the square, but not overwhelmingly so, with 17 out of 27 voting in favour. To provide a carrot as well as using sticks, the council asked English Heritage to assist with subsidies for the reinstatement of boundary walls.

At the same time, a radical solution was put forward: the creation of an underground car park. This proved to be a lengthy debate, and it was taken no further owing to the impact it would have had on the trees, the high cost and the effect on the square's overall character and appearance. In 1990 the Draft Local Plan was published, the first to cover the city centre area for more than 20 years. The council recognised

No. 17 Queen Square after end of forecourt parking and railings being brought back. [Bristol City Council]

Queen Square as a major open space of historic importance, and called for the closure of the road. It was now a flagship project of both the city and Avon County Council, who wanted to make practical progress in lessening the impact of the car. The project, uniquely, had the support of all political parties.

Change was certainly needed: Redcliffe Way was used by 20,000 vehicles each day. Success came quickly for once. In 1992, the main entrances to the square were closed to cars, though buses were still allowed through, using a one-way system round the perimeter of the square. This experiment was an overwhelming success, and the closure of the dual carriageway was made permanent in November 1993. There was also criticism about an increase in pollution and noise from the re-routed buses. Further improvements to nearby streets would be needed first before the buses could be removed altogether. Cars were still allowed access, with limited parking for permit holders during the day and for visitors at night.

In July 1992, a new plan to reinstate the square to its former status was published. The plan included the renovation of the statue, returning the forecourts to their original state and use, pedestrianisation, new signage and information points. This was superseded by a new local plan, which created the conditions for final work on the square. The case was now made and the will was there: all that was needed was the funding.

## The Transformation ■

A NEW EFFORT STARTED in the mid-1990s, led by Bristol City Council. Confidence was growing in the city. The demise of Avon County Council meant that Bristol was in more control of its own destiny. There was a new spirit of partnership in the city, with public and private sectors working together. The economy was growing, and new funding from the national lottery meant that projects which until now had been dreams could become reality – At-Bristol, the arts, nature and science facilities on the Harbourside, was but one example of a land-mark millennium project. The city had also led successfully some major renovation projects, Canon's Marsh being the most notable. The new phase of the regeneration of the docks had started, having been led some years earlier by the move of Arnolfini to Narrow Quay and the opening of the headquar-ters of Lloyds Bank. The restoration of Castle Park had created a new green space in the centre of the city near Bristol Bridge, where the city had first started. At the same time, closing the road in front of the Cathedral had provided a more appropri-ate setting not just for the Cathedral but also for the Council House. Finally, the city's conservation programme had for some time been tackling successfully the backlog of derelict historic properties and encouraging regeneration. The popu-larity of these projects provided further impetus for the restoration of Queen Square.

Considerable work was needed, though. It was not just the pollution and intrusion caused by buses: the area was not welcoming to pedestrians, the architectural integrity of the square was being compromised, and work was needed on both the trees and the statue. The square, in short, was a mess: pavements were a mixture of original pennant stone and concrete slabs; pavings and original setts had been covered with bitmac; for the mobility-impaired, parts of the square were dangerous; the pathway around the square was covered in tarmac. The original intention of a promenade, under the shade provided by trees, was impossible due to mud. Finally, signage was poor, and there was no historical interpretation on the streets, in one of the richest historical areas in the city. The square, as the city council said, was more to 'pass through, rather than walk around, linger in and enjoy'.[70]

There was also wide acceptance that the potential of the square was not being developed. The renewal of cities in the 1990s as places for work, play, living and learning demanded good public spaces. New city thinking said that such green

The courtyard restored at No. 38.
[Stephen Morris]

The paths reinstated.
[Stephen Morris]

spaces and squares were essential for prosperity. They were essential also for life: Louis Kahn, the architect, said that 'A city is a place where a small boy, as he walks through it, may see something that will tell him what he wants to do with his life.' Cities also needed places for contemplation. I quoted W H Davies' poem *Leisure* at the launch of At-Bristol, and one could apply this equally to Queen Square:

> *What is this life if, full of care,*
>
> *We have no time to stand and stare.*
>
> *No time to stand beneath the boughs*
>
> *And stare as long as sheep or cows.*
>
> *No time to see, when woods we pass,*
>
> *Where squirrels hide their nuts in grass.*
>
> *No time to see, in broad daylight,*
>
> *Streams full of stars like skies at night.*
>
> *No time to turn at Beauty's glance,*
>
> *And watch her feet, how they can dance.*
>
> *No time to wait till her mouth can*
>
> *Enrich that smile her eyes began.*
>
> *A poor life this if, full of care,*
>
> *We have no time to stand and stare.*

The aim was not to provide a restored square based on a

specific period, but the 're-integration of major historic features which have been consistent with the life of the Square'.[71] A return to the designs of 1710 and 1750, for example, might not include paths and would mean the removal of many mature trees. It was essential to take into account the needs of Bristol now and in the future. Car parking was needed, though it would be restricted; the wishes and needs of existing office users had to be considered, as well as those of pedestrians.

In the end, the National Heritage Lottery joined Bristol City Council and the Queen Square Association to pay for the restoration of the central part of the square in 2000. English Heritage covered the cost of work on the statue. The dual carriageway was removed and Rysbrack's statue was restored and floodlit. The wide gravel paths have now been restored. Tarmac has been removed from perimeter roads revealing the original setts. Gaps in the rows of trees have been filled with mature saplings. Roped walkways and stone pavements have been reinstated. New artworks have been commissioned, too, with eight artist-designed bird boxes placed in the trees. These reflect the history and ecology of the square, express contemporary concern about the loss of bird species in the

The setts revealed, 2001. [Stephen Morris]

One of eight bird boxes.
[Stephen Morris]

city centre and, perhaps, atone a little for the nests destroyed in 1837.

The official re-opening was held on 19 September 2000, 300 years after work first started on the square. The scheme showed that urban centres could be claimed back from the car: five months later, buses were no longer allowed to use the square, removing 1,200 journeys daily. A major public space was created – even the 'no ball games' signs were taken down in 2002. Queen Square had started as open land; it was now, once again, open land and people began to use the grassed areas in large numbers.

The scheme was popular, too, with those who worked there, despite much disruption. There remain minor points of dispute about the car (not all office workers, it should be said, are in favour of allowing more cars in the square – some want none at all) and there are concerns over security, especially at night, and the use of the square on a few occasions by drunks and drug addicts. Most, though, praise the develop-

ment. 'A delightful square,' said one company, adding 'we love it'. A 'beautiful square' another said. One claimed it to be 'the most attractive working environment in Bristol' with 'great ambience'. A company involved in legal work called it 'wonderful' and described 'a growing sense of community' in the square.[72]

Even the local media, not generally supportive of recent urban design initiatives in the city, backed the new square. In August 2002, the *Bristol Evening Post* called Queen Square 'a place where people want to go, not simply a place on the way to somewhere else'. They added, it 'stands today as a remarkable testament to vision and dedication, a clever and sensitive balance between reinstating a classic design and accommodating the needs of a modern city.'[73] As they said, it sets the standard.

King William III in the renewed Queen Square, 2003. [Stephen Morris]

## Final Thoughts ■

WALKING AROUND QUEEN SQUARE in July 2002, Howard
Jacobson, the novelist, came across the statue of William III
but found to his surprise – as he said, this is a quiet place
now – 'My name is Maureer. I hate you and all you stand for'
written on it.[74] He speculated that there was much to hate:
militarism, Protestant attacks on Catholics, the slave trade,
even that Maureer was a descendant of Van Oost and wanted
to take the creative credit for the statue. Maureer had a
point: there is much to dislike in Queen Square or at least to
learn about and remember. But it is a hatred for elements of
the past, one that has no place today. We should recognise
Queen Square for what it is and the remarkable creation of
beauty that it has become.

Often councils are attacked for inactivity, sometimes justi-
fiably so. Queen Square is an example where a local authority
has been bold. Rudolph Giuliani, on leaving his post as New
York Mayor in 2001, said that 'Civic leaders have a responsibility to leave cities far greater and more beautiful than they
were transmitted to us'. Those involved in the Queen Square
programme can rest assured that they have made a change by
creating a beautiful space, and helped build a better Bristol
for the future. In decades to come Bristolians, and those who
visit the city, will look back and thank those who created this
space. In an age of instant gratification and the quick fix, the
long-term solution was looked for, grasped and completed.

# Notes ■

1 Ivan Klima, 'How to Love a City', *Guardian Review*, 17 August 2002, p. 25.

2 Information provided by Jon Brett. See also 'The Costs of Queen Elizabeth's Visit to Bristol in August 1574', in McGrath, P, *A Bristol Miscellany*, Bristol: Bristol Record Society, 1985, pp. 6-12.

3 Exwood, M and Lehmann, HL, *The Journal of William Schellinks' Travels in England 1661-1663*, London: Offices of the Royal Historical Society, 1993, p.102

4 Morris, C, (ed.), *The Journeys of Celia Fiennes*, London: The Cresset Press, 1949, p. 238.

5 For a history of rope making see http://www.rope-maker.com/index.html.

6 Pepys, S, *A Diary of Samuel Pepys, 1668-9*, London: Bell & Hyman, 1976, p. 235.

7 Information from Borsay, P, *The English Urban Renaissance*, Oxford: Clarendon Press, 1989.

8 Quoted in Marcy, PT, *Eighteenth Century Views of Bristol and Bristolians*, Bristol: Bristol Branch of the Historical Association, p. 2.

9 Borsay, op. cit., p. 42.

10 Hughes, P and Root, J, *The History and Development of Queen Square*, unpublished manuscript, Bristol: Bristol City Council, p.8.

11 Dening, CFW, *The Eighteenth Century Architecture of Bristol*, Bristol: JW Arrowsmith, 1923, p. 37.

12 Ibid.

13 See Mowl, T, *To Build the Second City: architects and craftsmen of Georgian Bristol*, Bristol: Redcliffe Press, 1991, pp. 10-13.

14 Ison, W, *The Georgian Buildings of Bristol*, London: Faber and Faber, 1952, p. 143.

15 Reade was the Vicar of St Nicholas.

16 Ison, op. cit., p. 141.

17 Dening, op. cit., p. 37.

18 Mowl, op. cit., p. 11.

19 Ison, op. cit., p. 147.

20 Bristol Record Office, 04335 (8) f.254, in Hughes and Root, op. cit., p. 18.

21  Dresser, M, *Slavery Obscured: the social history of the slave trade in an English provincial port*, London: Continuum, 2001, p.107.

22  Quoted in Dening, op. cit., p. 37.

23  Ison, op. cit., p. 146.

24  Marcy, op. cit., p. 9.

25  For details, see Severin, T, 'Marooned', *American Scholar*, Summer 2002, pp. 73-82.

26  Ison, op. cit., pp. 148-149.

27  Mowl, op. cit., p. 13.

28  Merritt, D, *Sculpture in Bristol*, Bristol: Redcliffe Press, 2002, p. 16.

29  Quoted in ibid, p. 8.

30  Dening, op. cit., p. 37.

31  Bristol Record Office, 04264 (12), f. 116, in Hughes and Root, op. cit., p. 24.

32  Sherburn, G, (ed.), *Correspondence of Alexander Pope*, 1956, quoted in Bettey, JH, *Bristol Observed*, Bristol: Redcliffe Press, 1989, pp. 67-69.

33  Sansom, J, *Bristol First: city of discovery, invention and enterprise*, Bristol: Redcliffe Press, 1997, p. 48.

34  Marcy, op. cit., 10.

35  Barrett, W., *Barrett's History of Bristol*, Bristol, 1789, p. 85, quoted in Hughes and Root, p. 28.

36  Nicholls, JF, and Taylor, J, *Bristol Past and Present*, Bristol and London, 1881-2, vol. 3, p. 165, quoted in Dresser, op. cit., p. 97.

37  See Dresser, op. cit., p. 105.

38  See Hughes and Root, op. cit., p 9. For a detailed study of Bristol and riots see Phillips, JA, *The Great Reform Bill in the Boroughs: English electoral behaviour, 1818-1841*, Oxford: Clarendon Press, 1992, especially 'Reform and Reaction: Bristol and 1832', pp. 65-105; and Poole, S, 'To be a Bristolian: civic identity and the social order, 1750-1850', in Dresser, M and Ollerenshaw, P, *The Making of Modern Bristol*, Tiverton: Redcliffe Press, 1996, pp. 76-95.

39  Quoted in Poole, op. cit., p. 87.

40  Ibid, p. 95.

41 See Thomas, S, 'The Bristol Riots', Bristol: Bristol Branch of the Historical Association, reprint 1999, pp. 2-3.

42 Peter Macdonald's *Hotheads and Heroes: the Bristol Riots of 1831*, Bristol: Petmac Publications, 1995, a racy account of the riots, claims, based on an unreferenced newspaper report, that hundreds died. This is almost certainly inaccurate, though it is possible that the numbers of dead were more than those officially reported.

43 See Thomas, op. cit., and Hughes and Root, op. cit., p. 34.

44 Quoted in Sansom, op. cit., p. 49.

45 See Phillips, J A, op. cit.

46 See Poole, op. cit., p. 85.

47 Thomas, op. cit., p. 26.

48 Ibid, p. 12.

49 See Morgan, K, 'The Economic Development of Bristol, 1700-1850', in Dresser and Ollerenshaw, op. cit., p. 53.

50 See Phillips, op. cit., p. 66.

51 Quoted in ibid.

52 *Felix Farley's Bristol Journal*, 9 November 1831, quoted in Hughes and Root, op. cit., p. 34.

53 In *The Mansion House, Clifton*, Bristol: Redcliffe Press, 1993.

54 Thomas, op. cit., p. 5.

55 Quoted in Buchanan, A, *Brunel: the life and times of Isambard Kingdom Brunel*, London: Hambledon and London, 2002, p.51.

56 Details of this have been taken from Vaughan, A, *Isambard Kingdom Brunel: engineering knight-errant*, London: John Murray, 1991, p.40.

57 See Phillips, op. cit, p. 70.

58 See Poole, op. cit., p. 85.

59 See Harrison, M, 'Symbolism, "ritualism" and the location of crowds in early nineteenth-century English towns', in Cosgrove, D and Daniels, S, (ed), *The Iconography of Landscape: essays on the symbolic representation, design and use of past environments*, Cambridge: Cambridge University Press, 1988, pp. 194-204.

60 *Bristol Mercury*, 30 June 1832, quoted in ibid, p.199

61 Bristol Record Office, 04818 (2) pp. 126, 325, quoted in Hughes and Root, op. cit., p. 37.

62 Quoted in Hughes and Root, op. cit., p. 37.

63 See Cannon, J, 'The Chartists in Bristol', Bristol: Historical Association, 1964.

64 Dening, op. cit., p. 38.

65 Ison, op. cit., p. 147.

66 All quotations in this section come from personal reminiscences of those that lived in the square.

67 Betjeman, J, 'Bristol: an unspoiled city', in Green, CL, (ed.), *John Betjeman Coming Home: an anthology of his prose 1920-1977*, London: Methuen, 1997, p. 85.

68 Betjeman, in ibid, p.408.

69 Quoted in Hughes and Root, op. cit., p. 72.

70 Application to Heritage Lottery Fund, Bristol: Bristol City Council, nd, p.24

71 *The Restoration of Queen Square*, unpublished document, Bristol: Bristol City Council, p. 26

72 The quotes in this section come from comments made in responses to a questionnaire circulated in autumn 2002.

73 See 'Queen Square sets the standard', *Bristol Evening Post*, 5 August 2002.

74 Jacobson, H, 'Hate – it really is all the rage these days', The *Independent*, 6 July 2002.

# FORMUL

## ANNUAL 2011

Written by David Clayton
Designed by Simon Thorley
Dedicated to Jordan Cain

£7.99

# CONTENTS

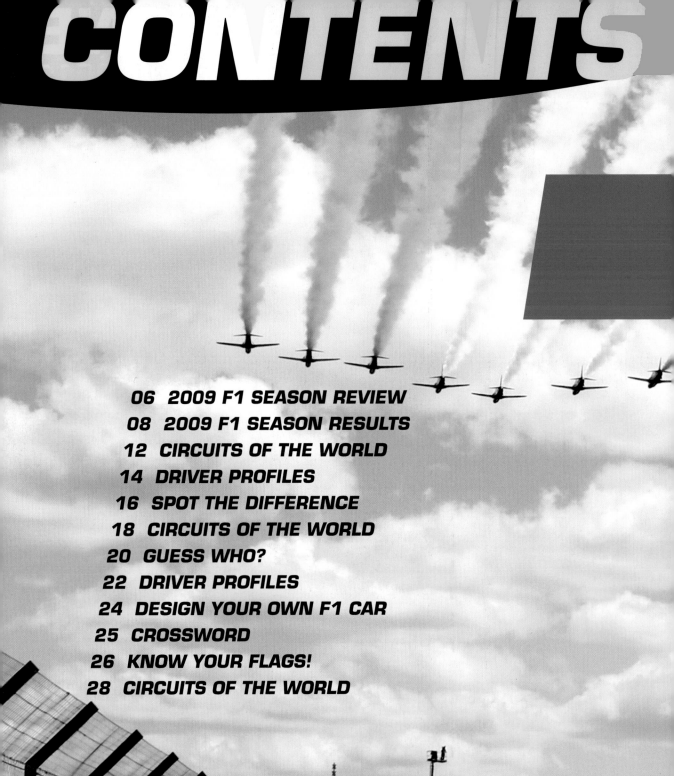

The 17 rounds of the Formula One World Championship began in Australia in March 2009 and ended in Abu Dhabi in November. It was an exciting, controversial and thrilling battle which ultimately saw a new champion crowned.

Suggestions of ways to make the new season more exciting included scrapping the points system and instead giving the championship to the driver with the most wins, but it was decided to leave things the way they were.

The Canadian and French Grands Prix were dropped and the new Abu Dhabi venue was included instead. Brawn GP were the newest team to enter the championship with Honda dropping out. Defending champion Lewis Hamilton was hoping to once again challenge for the title, but he soon discovered that new aerodynamics and tyres had left his team McLaren struggling in the early tests in Barcelona.

Some teams were having trouble adapting to new regulations and by the time they had caught up, the season was half over. Britain's Jenson Button had dreamed of one day winning

the world title, but his efforts had seen him only occasionally threaten to challenge the established leaders.

With a new car and a new team behind him, however, Button's dream was about to come true. Brawn made a stunning start to the 2009 season and Button, who had previously won just one Grand Prix, won six of the first seven races – it was incredible!

The points Button accumulated meant that even with 10 races remaining, if he remained steady and kept picking up points along the way, he would be in with a great chance of winning the title. In fact, the lack of a consistent challenger meant that despite Button failing to win any more races that season and only having two podium finishes in the last 10 races, he still won the championship by 11 points with Sebastian Vettel finishing second.

Lewis Hamilton finished fifth with 49 points – almost half Button's total – and Brawn also picked up the Constructor's Championship in their debut season.

**Well done Jenson!**

# 2009 FORMULA ONE SEASON RESULTS

## ABU DHABI
### YAS MARINA CIRCUIT, SUNDAY, 1 NOVEMBER 2009

| Position | Country | Driver | Car no: | Team | Grid | Race time | Points |
|---|---|---|---|---|---|---|---|
| 1 | Germany | Sebastian Vettel | 15 | Red Bull-Renault | 2 | 1:34:03.414 | 10 |
| 2 | Australia | Mark Webber | 14 | Red Bull-Renault | 3 | 1:34:21.271 | 8 |
| 3 | Great Britain | Jenson Button | 22 | Brawn-Mercedes | 5 | 1:34:21.881 | 6 |

## BRAZIL
### INTERLAGOS, SUNDAY, 18 OCTOBER 2009

| Position | Country | Driver | Car no: | Team | Grid | Race time | Points |
|---|---|---|---|---|---|---|---|
| 1 | Australia | Mark Webber | 14 | Red Bull-Renault | 2 | 1:32:23.081 | 10 |
| 2 | Poland | Robert Kubica | 5 | BMW Sauber | 8 | 1:32:30.707 | 8 |
| 3 | Great Britain | Lewis Hamilton | 1 | McLaren-Mercedes | 17 | 1:32:42.025 | 6 |

## JAPAN
### SUZUKA, SUNDAY, 4 OCTOBER 2009

| Position | Country | Driver | Car no: | Team | Grid | Race time | Points |
|---|---|---|---|---|---|---|---|
| 1 | Germany | Sebastian Vettel | 15 | Red Bull-Renault | 1 | 1:28:20.443 | 10 |
| 2 | Italy | Jarno Trulli | 9 | Toyota | 2 | 1:28:25.243 | 8 |
| 3 | Great Britain | Lewis Hamilton | 1 | McLaren-Mercedes | 3 | 1:28:26.843 | 6 |

## SINGAPORE
### SINGAPORE, SUNDAY, 27 SEPTEMBER 2009

| Position | Country | Driver | Car no: | Team | Grid | Race time | Points |
|---|---|---|---|---|---|---|---|
| 1 | Great Britain | Lewis Hamilton | 1 | McLaren-Mercedes | 1 | 1:56:06.337 | 10 |
| 2 | Germany | Timo Glock | 10 | Toyota | 6 | 1:56:18.971 | 8 |
| 3 | Spain | Fernando Alonso | 7 | Renault | 5 | 1:56:22.961 | 6 |

## ITALY
### MONZA, SUNDAY, 13 SEPTEMBER 2009

| Position | Country | Driver | Car no: | Team | Grid | Race time | Points |
|---|---|---|---|---|---|---|---|
| 1 | Brazil | Rubens Barrichello | 23 | Brawn-Mercedes | 5 | 1:16:21.706 | 10 |
| 2 | Great Britain | Jenson Button | 22 | Brawn-Mercedes | 6 | 1:16:24.572 | 8 |
| 3 | Finland | Kimi Räikkönen | 4 | Ferrari | 3 | 1:16:52.370 | 6 |

## BELGIUM
### SPA-FRANCORCHAMPS, SUNDAY, 30 AUGUST 2009

| Position | Country | Driver | Car no: | Team | Grid | Race time | Points |
|---|---|---|---|---|---|---|---|
| 1 | Finland | Kimi Räikkönen | 4 | Ferrari | 6 | 1:23:50.995 | 10 |
| 2 | Italy | Giancarlo Fisichella | 21 | Force India-Mercedes | 1 | 1:23:51.934 | 8 |
| 3 | Germany | Sebastian Vettel | 15 | Red Bull-Renault | 8 | 1:23:54.870 | 6 |

## EUROPE
### VALENCIA, SUNDAY, 23 AUGUST 2009

| Position | Country | Driver | Car no: | Team | Grid | Race time | Points |
|---|---|---|---|---|---|---|---|
| 1 | Brazil | Rubens Barrichello | 23 | Brawn-Mercedes | 3 | 1:35:51.289 | 10 |
| 2 | Great Britain | Lewis Hamilton | 1 | McLaren-Mercedes | 1 | 1:35:53.647 | 8 |
| 3 | Finland | Kimi Räikkönen | 4 | Ferrari | 6 | 1:36:07.283 | 6 |

## HUNGARY
### HUNGARORING, SUNDAY, 26 JULY 2009

| Position | Country | Driver | Car no: | Team | Grid | Race time | Points |
|---|---|---|---|---|---|---|---|
| 1 | Great Britain | Lewis Hamilton | 1 | McLaren-Mercedes | 4 | 1:38:23.876 | 10 |
| 2 | Finland | Kimi Räikkönen | 4 | Ferrari | 7 | 1:38:34.881 | 8 |
| 3 | Australia | Mark Webber | 14 | Red Bull-Renault | 3 | 1:38:39.884 | 6 |

## GERMANY
### NÜRBURGRING, SUNDAY, 12 JULY 2009

| Position | Country | Driver | Car no: | Team | Grid | Race time | Points |
|---|---|---|---|---|---|---|---|
| 1 | Australia | Mark Webber | 14 | Red Bull-Renault | 1 | 1:36:43.310 | 10 |
| 2 | Germany | Sebastian Vettel | 15 | Red Bull-Renault | 4 | 1:36:52.562 | 8 |
| 3 | Brazil | Felipe Massa | 3 | Ferrari | 8 | 1:36:59.216 | 6 |

## GREAT BRITAIN
### SILVERSTONE, SUNDAY, 21 JUNE 2009

| Position | Country | Driver | Car no: | Team | Grid | Race time | Points |
|---|---|---|---|---|---|---|---|
| 1 | Germany | Sebastian Vettel | 15 | Red Bull-Renault | 1 | 1:22:49.328 | 10 |
| 2 | Australia | Mark Webber | 14 | Red Bull-Renault | 3 | 1:23:04.516 | 8 |
| 3 | Brazil | Rubens Barrichello | 23 | Brawn-Mercedes | 2 | 1:23:30.483 | 6 |

## TURKEY
### ISTANBUL, SUNDAY, 7 JUNE 2009

| Position | Country | Driver | Car no: | Team | Grid | Race time | Points |
|---|---|---|---|---|---|---|---|
| 1 | Great Britain | Jenson Button | 22 | Brawn-Mercedes | 2 | 1:26:24.848 | 10 |
| 2 | Australia | Mark Webber | 14 | Red Bull-Renault | 4 | 1:26:31.562 | 8 |
| 3 | Germany | Sebastian Vettel | 15 | Red Bull-Renault | 1 | 1:26:32.309 | 6 |

## MONACO
### MONTE CARLO, SUNDAY, 24 MAY 2009

| Position | Country | Driver | Car no: | Team | Grid | Race time | Points |
|---|---|---|---|---|---|---|---|
| 1 | Great Britain | Jenson Button | 22 | Brawn-Mercedes | 1 | 1:40:44.282 | 10 |
| 2 | Brazil | Rubens Barrichello | 23 | Brawn-Mercedes | 3 | 1:40:51.948 | 8 |
| 3 | Finland | Kimi Räikkönen | 4 | Ferrari | 2 | 1:40:57.724 | 6 |

# 2009 FORMULA ONE SEASON RESULTS

## SPAIN
### BARCELONA, SUNDAY, 10 MAY 2009

| Position | Country | Driver | Car no: | Team | Grid | Race time | Points |
|---|---|---|---|---|---|---|---|
| 1 | Great Britain | Jenson Button | 22 | Brawn-Mercedes | 1 | 1:37:19.202 | 10 |
| 2 | Brazil | Rubens Barrichello | 23 | Brawn-Mercedes | 3 | 1:37:32.258 | 8 |
| 3 | Australia | Mark Webber | 14 | Red Bull-Renault | 5 | 1:37:33.126 | 6 |

## BAHRAIN
### SAKHIR, SUNDAY, 26 APRIL 2009

| Position | Country | Driver | Car no: | Team | Grid | Race time | Points |
|---|---|---|---|---|---|---|---|
| 1 | Great Britain | Jenson Button | 22 | Brawn-Mercedes | 4 | 1:31:48.182 | 10 |
| 2 | Germany | Sebastian Vettel | 15 | Red Bull-Renault | 3 | 1:31:55.369 | 8 |
| 3 | Italy | Jarno Trulli | 9 | Toyota | 1 | 1:31:57.352 | 6 |

## CHINA
### SHANGHAI, SUNDAY, 19 APRIL 2009

| Position | Country | Driver | Car no: | Team | Grid | Race time | Points |
|---|---|---|---|---|---|---|---|
| 1 | Germany | Sebastian Vettel | 15 | Red Bull-Renault | 1 | 1:57:43.485 | 10 |
| 2 | Australia | Mark Webber | 14 | Red Bull-Renault | 3 | 1:57:54.455 | 8 |
| 3 | Great Britain | Jenson Button | 22 | Brawn-Mercedes | 5 | 1:58:28.460 | 6 |

## MALAYSIA
### SEPANG, SUNDAY, 5 APRIL 2009

| Position | Country | Driver | Car no: | Team | Grid | Race time | Points |
|---|---|---|---|---|---|---|---|
| 1 | Great Britain | Jenson Button | 22 | Brawn-Mercedes | 1 | 0:55:30.622 | 5 |
| 2 | Germany | Nick Heidfeld | 6 | BMW Sauber | 10 | 0:55:53.344 | 4 |
| 3 | Germany | Timo Glock | 10 | Toyota | 3 | 0:55:54.135 | 3 |

## AUSTRALIA
### ALBERT PARK, SUNDAY, 29 MARCH 2009

| Position | Country | Driver | Car no: | Team | Grid | Race time | Points |
|---|---|---|---|---|---|---|---|
| 1 | Great Britain | Jenson Button | 22 | Brawn-Mercedes | 1 | 1:34:15.784 | 10 |
| 2 | Brazil | Rubens Barrichello | 23 | Brawn-Mercedes | 2 | 1:34:16.591 | 8 |
| 3 | Italy | Jarno Trulli | 9 | Toyota | 19 | 1:34:17.384 | 6 |

# 2009 FORMULA ONE SEASON RESULTS

## F1 DRIVERS' CHAMPIONSHIP FINAL STANDINGS 2009

| | Driver | Team | Points |
|---|---|---|---|
| 1 | Jenson Button | Brawn-Mercedes | 95 |
| 2 | Sebastian Vettel | Red Bull-Renault | 84 |
| 3 | Rubens Barrichello | Brawn-Mercedes | 77 |
| 4 | Mark Webber | Red Bull-Renault | 69.5 |
| 5 | Lewis Hamilton | McLaren-Mercedes | 49 |
| 6 | Kimi Räikkönen | Ferrari | 48 |
| 7 | Nico Rosberg | Williams-Toyota | 34.5 |
| 8 | Jarno Trulli | Toyota | 32.5 |
| 9 | Fernando Alonso | Renault | 26 |
| 10 | Timo Glock | Toyota | 24 |
| 11 | Felipe Massa | Ferrari | 22 |
| 12 | Heikki Kovalainen | McLaren-Mercedes | 22 |
| 13 | Nick Heidfeld | BMW Sauber | 19 |
| 14 | Robert Kubica | BMW Sauber | 17 |
| 15 | Giancarlo Fisichella | Ferrari | 8 |
| 16 | Sébastien Buemi | STR-Ferrari | 6 |
| 17 | Adrian Sutil | Force India-Mercedes | 5 |
| 18 | Kamui Kobayashi | Toyota | 3 |
| 19 | Sébastien Bourdais | STR-Ferrari | 2 |
| =20 | Romain Grosjean | Renault | 0 |
| =20 | Vitantonio Liuzzi | Force India-Mercedes | 0 |
| =20 | Jaime Alguersuari | STR-Ferrari | 0 |
| =20 | Kazuki Nakajima | Williams-Toyota | 0 |
| =20 | Luca Badoer | Ferrari | 0 |
| =20 | Nelson Piquet Jnr | Renault | 0 |

## CONSTRUCTORS' CHAMPIONSHIP

| | Driver | Points |
|---|---|---|
| 1 | Brawn-Mercedes | 172 |
| 2 | Red Bull-Renault | 153.5 |
| 3 | McLaren-Mercedes | 71 |
| 4 | Ferrari | 70 |
| 5 | Toyota | 59.5 |
| 6 | BMW Sauber | 36 |
| 7 | Williams-Toyota | 34.5 |
| 8 | Renault | 26 |
| 9 | Force India-Mercedes | 13 |
| 10 | STR-Ferrari | 8 |

# F1WORLDCIRCUITS

## ABU DHABI GRAND PRIX
### YAS MARINA CIRCUIT, YAS ISLAND, ABU DHABI

FIRST RACE: 2009
CIRCUIT LENGTH: 5.522 KM
LAPS: 55
BUILT: 2009
CAPACITY: 41,093

## AUSTRALIAN GRAND PRIX
### ALBERT PARK, MELBOURNE

FIRST RACE: 1996
CIRCUIT LENGTH: 5.272 KM
LAPS: 58
BUILT: 1996
CAPACITY: 80,000
RECORD CROWD: 300,000 (OVER 4 DAYS)

# BAHRAIN GRAND PRIX
## BAHRAIN INTERNATIONAL RACING CIRCUIT, SAKHIR

FIRST RACE: 2004
CIRCUIT LENGTH: 5.381 KM
LAPS: 57
BUILT: 2003/2004
CAPACITY: 50,000
RECORD CROWD: 24,000 (IN 2008)

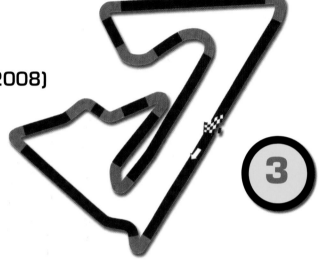

# BELGIAN GRAND PRIX
## SPA FRANCORCHAMPS CIRCUIT, FRANCORCHAMPS

FIRST RACE: 1983 (REVISED SHORTER VERSION)
CIRCUIT LENGTH: 6.963 KM
LAPS: 44
BUILT: 1924 (STREET CIRCUIT)
CAPACITY: APPROX 90,000 (STREET CIRCUIT)
RECORD CROWD: 150,000 (OVER 3 DAYS)

## JAIME ALGUERSUARI

**TEAM:** TORO ROSSO
**BORN:** 23/03/1990
**NATIONALITY:** SPANISH
**BIRTHPLACE:** BARCELONA, SPAIN
**WORLD CHAMPIONSHIPS:** 0
**HIGHEST FINISH:** 9
**RACE WINS:** 0
**TOTAL POINTS:** 3

## FERNANDO ALONSO

**TEAM:** FERRARI
**BORN:** 29/07/1981
**NATIONALITY:** SPANISH
**BIRTHPLACE:** OVIEDO, SPAIN
**WORLD CHAMPIONSHIPS:** 2
**HIGHEST FINISH:** 1
**RACE WINS:** 23
**TOTAL POINTS:** 700

# RUBENS BARRICHELLO

**TEAM:** *WILLIAMS*
**BORN:** *23/05/1972*
**NATIONALITY:** *BRAZILIAN*
**BIRTHPLACE:** *SAO PAULO, BRAZIL*
**WORLD CHAMPIONSHIPS:** *0*
**HIGHEST FINISH:** *1*
**RACE WINS:** *11*
**TOTAL POINTS:** *636*

# SÉBASTIEN BUEMI

**TEAM:** *TORO ROSSO*
**BORN:** *31/10/1988*
**NATIONALITY:** *SWISS*
**BIRTHPLACE:** *AIGLE, SWITZERLAND*
**WORLD CHAMPIONSHIPS:** *0*
**HIGHEST FINISH:** *7*
**RACE WINS:** *0*
**TOTAL POINTS:** *13*

DETAILS CORRECT TO 31/07/10

# SPOT THE DIFFERENCE

PICTURE A AND B ARE THE SAME – OR ARE THEY? CAN YOU SPOT
AND CIRCLE THE SIX DIFFERENCES IN PICTURE B?

## BRAZILIAN GRAND PRIX
### AUTODROMO JOSE CARLOS PACE, SAO PAULO

FIRST RACE: 1973
CIRCUIT LENGTH: 4.283 KM
LAPS: 71
BUILT: 1940
CAPACITY: 80,000

## BRITISH GRAND PRIX
### SILVERSTONE CIRCUIT, NORTHANTS

FIRST RACE: 1950
CIRCUIT LENGTH: 5.110 KM
LAPS: 60
BUILT: 1948
CAPACITY: 90,000
RECORD CROWD: 310,000
(OVER 3 DAYS) IN 2009

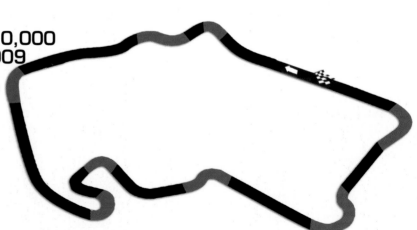

# CANADIAN GRAND PRIX
## CIRCUIT GILLES VILLENEUVE, MONTREAL

FIRST RACE: 1978
CIRCUIT LENGTH: 4.336 KM
LAPS: 70
BUILT: 1978
CAPACITY: 100,000
RECORD CROWD: 100,000

# CHINESE GRAND PRIX
## SHANGHAI CIRCUIT, SHANGHAI

FIRST RACE: 2004
CIRCUIT LENGTH: 5.419 KM
LAPS: 56
BUILT: 2003/2004
CAPACITY: 200,000

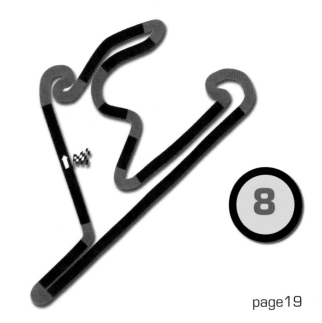

# GUESS WHO?

HERE ARE FOUR IMAGES OF SOME CURRENT F1 STARS, CAN YOU GUESS WHO THEY ARE?

Answers on page 60/61

## JENSON BUTTON

**TEAM:** MCLAREN
**BORN:** 19/01/1980
**NATIONALITY:** BRITISH
**BIRTHPLACE:** FROME, UK
**WORLD CHAMPIONSHIPS:** 1
**HIGHEST FINISH:** 1
**RACE WINS:** 9
**TOTAL POINTS:** 470

## KARUN CHANDHOK

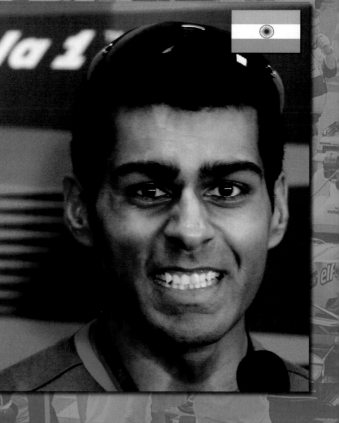

**TEAM:** HRT
**BORN:** 19/01/1984
**NATIONALITY:** INDIAN
**BIRTHPLACE:** CHENNAI, INDIA
**WORLD CHAMPIONSHIPS:** 0
**HIGHEST FINISH:** 14
**RACE WINS:** 0
**TOTAL POINTS:** 0

# TIMO GLOCK

**TEAM:** *VIRGIN*
**BORN:** *18/03/1982*
**NATIONALITY:** *GERMAN*
**BIRTHPLACE:** *LINDENFELS, GERMANY*
**WORLD CHAMPIONSHIPS:** *0*
**HIGHEST FINISH:** *2*
**RACE WINS:** *0*
**TOTAL POINTS:** *51*

# LUCAS DI GRASSI

**TEAM:** *VIRGIN*
**BORN:** *11/08/1984*
**NATIONALITY:** *BRAZILIAN*
**BIRTHPLACE:** *SAO PAULO, BRAZIL*
**WORLD CHAMPIONSHIPS:** *0*
**HIGHEST FINISH:** *14*
**RACE WINS:** *0*
**TOTAL POINTS:** *0*

# DESIGN YOUR OWN F1 CAR

WE'VE STRIPPED AN F1 CAR OF ITS DESIGN SO YOU CAN PUT YOUR OWN COLOURS ON – THE MORE STRIKING THE BETTER!

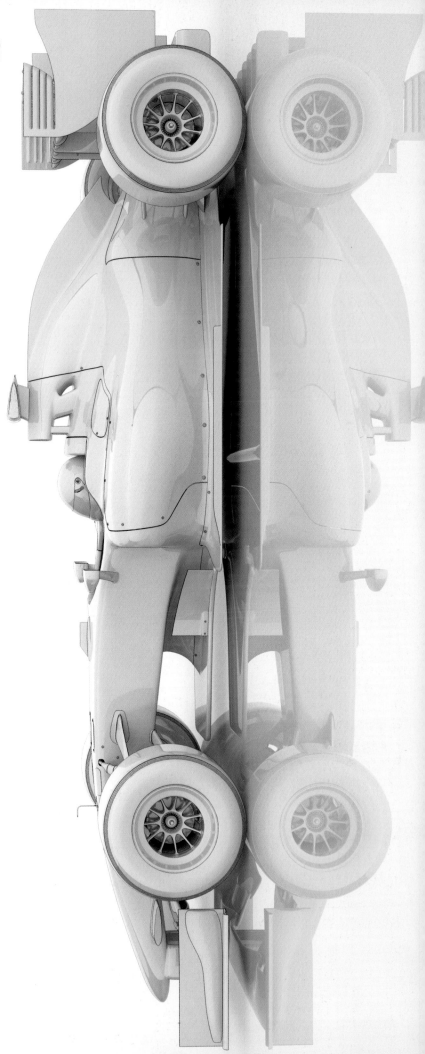

# F1 CROSSWORD

READ THE CLUES AND PUT THE ANSWERS INTO THE CROSSWORD PUZZLE. SEE IF YOU CAN FILL EVERY BLANK IN THE BOX!

## ACROSS

1 German driver now with Virgin (4,5)
2 Where every driver wants to start the race from (4,8)
6 This is held in front of a driver during a pit-stop - though he can't eat it! (8)
8 Electric blanket that is wrapped around the wheels prior to races (4,6)
9 Nationality of Jarno Trulli (7)
11 High ranking official employed at a Grand Prix to make important decisions (7)
12 Tight sequence of corners with alternate directions (7)
14 Race marshals will wave this if there is danger on the track (6,4)
17 A drink the winning drivers often spray on those who finish second and third (9)
18 Drivers prefer these when it rains (3,5)

## DOWN

1 What the winning driver is awarded (3,6)
3 Location of British Grand Prix (11)
4 Indian driver who drives for HRT (5,8)
5 Vitantonio Liuzzi drives for this team (5,5)
7 Area drivers must head for if given a drive through penalty (3,4)
10 The slowest car on the track that is often seen out in front! (6,3)
12 Where the driver sits (7)
13 A top three finish will ensure a place on this (6)
15 Country Robert Kubica was born in (6)
16 Every driver must wear one of these (6)

Solution on page 60/61

# KNOW YOUR FLAGS!

MANY TRACKSIDE FLAGS CAN BE SEEN WAVING DURING A RACE – BUT DO YOU KNOW WHAT THEY ARE FOR? HERE IS OUR GUIDE TO F1 FLAGS SO THAT THE NEXT TIME YOU'RE WATCHING A RACE, YOU'LL KNOW EXACTLY WHAT THEY MEAN AND WHY THEY ARE BEING WAVED....

### CHEQUERED FLAG

This is the most distinctive and famous of all the Grand Prix flags. When you see this being waved it indicates to drivers that the session has ended. It is shown first to the winner and then to every car that crosses the line behind him and means 'race over'!

### YELLOW FLAG

Yellow, in this case, means danger. It could be a stranded car ahead or some other potential problem for drivers. A single waved yellow flag warns drivers to slow down, while two waved yellow flags at the same post means that drivers must slow down and be prepared to stop if necessary. Overtaking at this point is prohibited for obvious reasons.

### GREEN FLAG

The green flag is a positive for drivers – it basically means 'all clear'. The driver has now passed the potential danger point and restrictions imposed by yellow flags have been lifted.

### RED FLAG

If the red flag is waved, it is usually because the session has been stopped, usually due to an accident or poor track conditions. Either way, it's time to stop!

### BLUE FLAG

It may mean a clean beach if you are by the seaside, but at an F1 race, the blue flag is waved to warn a driver that he is about to be lapped and to let the faster car overtake. Pass three blue flags without complying and drivers risks being penalised. Blue lights are also displayed at the end of the pit lane when the pit exit is open and a car on track is approaching – handy to know given the speed cars reach during the race.

### YELLOW AND RED STRIPED FLAG

This warns drivers of a slippery track surface, usually due to oil or water.

### BLACK WITH ORANGE CIRCLE FLAG

Accompanied by a car number, it warns a driver that he has a mechanical problem and must return to his pit – if you see this flag being waved at you, your number is literally up!

### HALF BLACK, HALF WHITE FLAG

Not a popular flag for drivers to see when accompanied by their car number because it means the stewards believe they've been guilty of unsporting behaviour. If the warning is heeded, it may be followed by a black flag...

### BLACK FLAG

Again, as you might imagine given the colour, when accompanied by a car number, it directs a driver to return to his pit and is most often used to signal to the driver that he has been excluded from the race. Not a good flag to see!

### WHITE FLAG

This is not a sign of surrender – just a warning that a slow moving vehicle is on the track.

## EUROPEAN GRAND PRIX (SPAIN)
### STREET CIRCUIT, VALENCIA

FIRST RACE: 2008
CIRCUIT LENGTH: 5.387 KM
LAPS: 57
BUILT: 2008 (STREET CIRCUIT)
CAPACITY: 112,771

**9**

## GERMAN GRAND PRIX
### HOCKENHEIMRING, HOCKENHEIM

FIRST RACE: 2002 (AS A NEW TRACK)
CIRCUIT LENGTH: 4.547 KM
LAPS: 67
BUILT: 2002
CAPACITY: 120,000

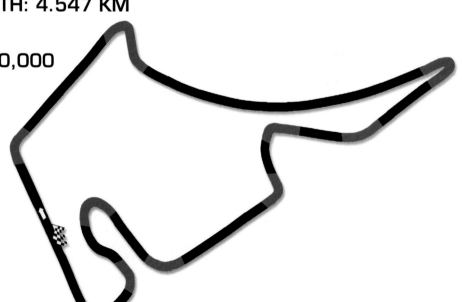

**10**

# HUNGARIAN GRAND PRIX
## HUNGARORING CIRCUIT, BUDAPEST

FIRST RACE: 1986
CIRCUIT LENGTH: 4.355 KM
LAPS: 70
BUILT: 1986
CAPACITY: 120,000
RECORD CROWD: 200,000
(OVER 3 DAYS) IN 2008

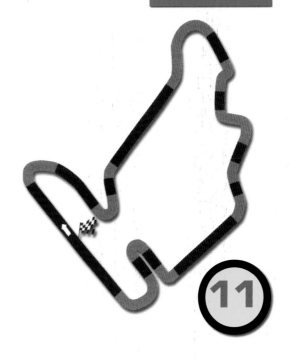

**11**

# ITALIAN GRAND PRIX
## MONZA CIRCUIT, MONZA

FIRST RACE: 1950
CIRCUIT LENGTH: 5.760 KM
LAPS: 53
BUILT: 1950
CAPACITY: 115,000
RECORD CROWD: 100,000

**12**

# IMAGINE IF...

## FERNANDO ALONSO DROVE ANY OF THESE OLD BANGERS...

HE'S ONE OF THE GREATEST F1 DRIVERS IN THE WORLD, BUT HOW WOULD HE PERFORM IF HE WAS FORCED TO DRIVE SOME OF THESE ALTERNATIVE MODES OF TRANSPORT...

THE THREE WHEELER

NODDY CAR

THE BATMOBILE

F1 UNPLUGGED

FERNANDO THE FASTEST
MILKMAN IN THE WEST

MUNSTER TRUCKS

# LOOKWHO'STALKING

WE DON'T KNOW FOR SURE WHAT THE DRIVERS WERE SAYING AT THE TIME THESE PICTURES WERE TAKEN – BUT WE CAN MAKE A PRETTY GOOD GUESS!

**A** "I KNOW I SAID DRIVING F1 WAS CHILD'S PLAY BUT LOOK AT MY DRESSING ROOM!"

**B** "CAN SOMEONE TELL THE DRIVER THIS IS A PIT-STOP, NOT A BUS-STOP!"

**C** "I TOLD YOU, NO EGG ON MY BACON SARNIE!"

**D** "MICHAEL, THIS SHOOT-OUT COULD CREATE HISTORY…"

"I KNOW SEB – AT LAST A GERMAN WILL ACTUALLY GET BEAT ON PENALTIES!"

# F1 WORDSEARCH

CAN YOU SPOT 10 F1 DRIVERS IN THE WORDSEARCH BELOW? REMEMBER, THE NAMES COULD BE IN ANY DIRECTION.

```
M Q X K K L N P N Z D B F C M
G R E B S O R O C I N E M N K
V R J M F R M Z Y K L V O Y C
I L E W I S H A M I L T O N O
T K L L T L K B P L T N L N L
A R R N B T L E Q U D R N I G
L E H H T R M U B R N K T B O
Y B K T M A U N R L Z U Y M M
P B M X S L O N G T S L N M I
E E Q S P S G N O N O L V T T
T W A H N C R N A S L N R R C
R K L E W Q P I D M E N R J N
O R J T L H R M W G G N T A X
V A D W Q D M G L D H R N G J
N M J M A R F V N L H H Q A M
```

FORZA FERRARI LA PLATA ARGENTINA

## LEWIS HAMILTON

**TEAM:** MCLAREN
**BORN:** 07/01/1985
**NATIONALITY:** BRITISH
**BIRTHPLACE:** STEVENAGE, UK
**WORLD CHAMPIONSHIPS:** 1
**HIGHEST FINISH:** 1
**RACE WINS:** 13
**TOTAL POINTS:** 413

## NICO HULKENBERG

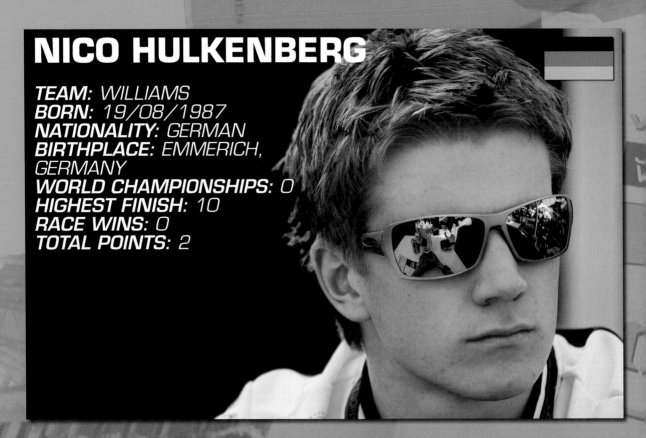

**TEAM:** WILLIAMS
**BORN:** 19/08/1987
**NATIONALITY:** GERMAN
**BIRTHPLACE:** EMMERICH, GERMANY
**WORLD CHAMPIONSHIPS:** 0
**HIGHEST FINISH:** 10
**RACE WINS:** 0
**TOTAL POINTS:** 2

# KAMUI KOBAYASHI

**TEAM:** *BMW SAUBER*
**BORN:** *13/09/1986*
**NATIONALITY:** *JAPANESE*
**BIRTHPLACE:** *AMAGASAKI, JAPAN*
**WORLD CHAMPIONSHIPS:** *0*
**HIGHEST FINISH:** *6*
**RACE WINS:** *0*
**TOTAL POINTS:** *18*

# HEIKKI KOVALAINEN

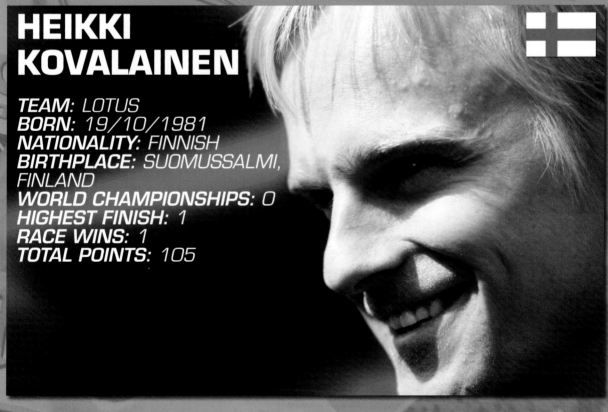

**TEAM:** *LOTUS*
**BORN:** *19/10/1981*
**NATIONALITY:** *FINNISH*
**BIRTHPLACE:** *SUOMUSSALMI, FINLAND*
**WORLD CHAMPIONSHIPS:** *0*
**HIGHEST FINISH:** *1*
**RACE WINS:** *1*
**TOTAL POINTS:** *105*

## JAPANESE GRAND PRIX
### SUZUKA, MIE PREFECTURE, JAPAN

FIRST RACE: 1962
CIRCUIT LENGTH: 5.773 KM
LAPS: 53
BUILT: 1962
CAPACITY: 100,000
RECORD CROWD: 100,000

## MALAYSIAN GRAND PRIX
### SEPANG INTERNATIONAL CIRCUIT, KUALA LUMPUR

FIRST RACE: 1999
CIRCUIT LENGTH: 5.510 KM
LAPS: 56
BUILT: 1998
CAPACITY: 130,000
RECORD CROWD: 115,794

# MONACO GRAND PRIX
## CIRCUIT DE MONACO, MONTE CARLO

FIRST RACE: 1950
CIRCUIT LENGTH: 3.320 KM
LAPS: 78
BUILT: 1950 (STREET CIRCUIT)
CAPACITY: 50,000

**15**

# SINGAPORE
## MARINA BAY, SINGAPORE

FIRST RACE: 2008
CIRCUIT LENGTH: 5.037 KM
LAPS: 61
BUILT: 2008 (STREET CIRCUIT)
CAPACITY: 100,000
RECORD CROWD:
100,000 IN 2008

**16**

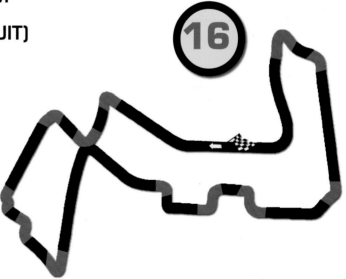

# THE BIG F1 QUIZ

**1, WHO IS THIS?**

**2, WHICH DRIVER HAS JUST WON A GRAND PRIX IN THIS PICTURE?**

**3, NAME FIVE GERMAN F1 DRIVERS.**

**4, WHAT IS THIS GUY'S JOB TITLE?**

**5, WHICH TEAM DID JENSON BUTTON WIN THE 2009 DRIVERS' CHAMPIONSHIP WITH?**

**6, WHICH COUNTRY IS VITALY PETROV FROM?**

**7, HOW MANY CHAMPIONSHIPS HAS MICHAEL SCHUMACHER WON?**

**8, WHICH TWO GRAND PRIX CIRCUITS WERE DROPPED IN 2009?**

**9, WHERE IS THIS?**

**10,** CAN YOU WORK OUT WHO
THIS IS?

**11,** WHAT DO THE SINGAPORE AND
MONACO GRAND PRIX HAVE IN
COMMON?

**12,** WHO SUFFERED A NASTY EYE
INJURY DURING THE 2009
SEASON, THREATENING HIS
CAREER?

**13,** WHAT WAS SO SPECIAL ABOUT
THE 2009 F1 SEASON?

**14,** WHO'S NAME IS THIS AN
ANAGRAM OF – SON RICE BOG?

**15,** WHO IS THIS?

**16,** WHERE DID LEWIS HAMILTON
FINISH IN THE 2010 BRITISH
GRAND PRIX?

**17,** HOW MANY WORLD
CHAMPIONSHIPS HAS
FERNANDO ALONSO WON?

**18,** WHICH F1 TEAM DO YOU
ASSOCIATE THIS IMAGE WITH?

**19,** CAN YOU IDENTIFY THIS F1
DRIVER?

**20,** THOUGH HE RETURNED FOR THE
2010 SEASON, WHICH YEAR DID
MICHAEL SCHUMACHER
ORIGINALLY RETIRE?
A) 2005 B) 2006 C) 2007

Answers on page 60/61

# WHICHCIRCUIT?

YOU'D HAVE TO BE AN F1 EXPERT TO GET ALL THESE RIGHT – SEE IF YOU CAN WORK OUT AT WHICH CIRCUITS THE IMAGES BELOW WERE TAKEN…

A

B

C

D

Answers on page 60/61

# AUTOGRAPHPLEASE!

EVER WONDERED HOW YOUR FAVOURITE DRIVER SIGNS HIS NAME?
BELOW, WE'VE MANAGED TO COLLECT A FEW AUTOGRAPHS TO
FIND OUT WHO HAS STYLE AND WHO JUST SCRIBBLES!

**SCHUMACHER**

**WEBBER**

**BUTTON**

**MASSA**

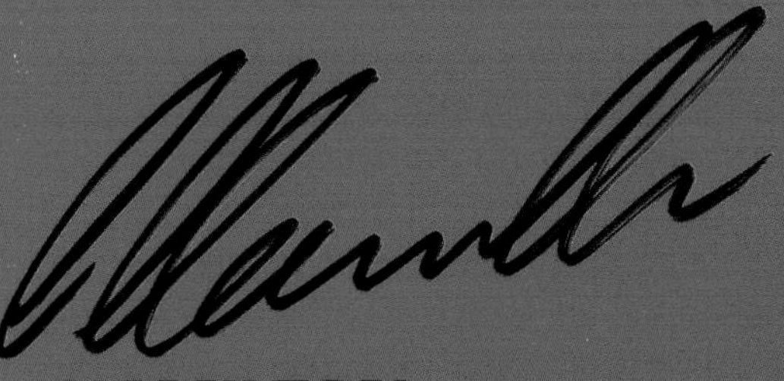

**HAMILTON**

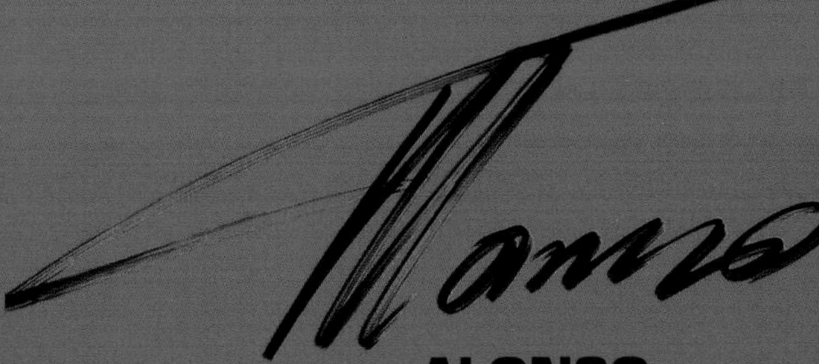

**ALONSO**

**TRULLI**

## ROBERT KUBICA

**TEAM:** RENAULT
**BORN:** 07/12/1984
**NATIONALITY:** POLISH
**BIRTHPLACE:** KRAKOW, POLAND
**WORLD CHAMPIONSHIPS:** 0
**HIGHEST FINISH:** 1
**RACE WINS:** 1
**TOTAL POINTS:** 226

## VITANTONIO LIUZZI

**TEAM:** FORCE INDIA
**BORN:** 06/08/1981
**NATIONALITY:** ITALIAN
**BIRTHPLACE:** LOCOROTONDO, ITALY
**WORLD CHAMPIONSHIPS:** 0
**HIGHEST FINISH:** 6
**RACE WINS:** 0
**TOTAL POINTS:** 17

# FELIPE
# MASSA

**TEAM:** FERRARI
**BORN:** 25/04/1981
**NATIONALITY:** BRAZILIAN
**BIRTHPLACE:** SAO PAULO,
BRAZIL
**WORLD CHAMPIONSHIPS:** 0
**HIGHEST FINISH:** 1
**RACE WINS:** 11
**TOTAL POINTS:** 405

# VITALY
# PETROV

**TEAM:** RENAULT
**BORN:** 08/09/1984
**NATIONALITY:** RUSSIAN
**BIRTHPLACE:** VYBORG,
RUSSIA
**WORLD CHAMPIONSHIPS:** 0
**HIGHEST FINISH:** 7
**RACE WINS:** 0
**TOTAL POINTS:** 7

DETAILS CORRECT TO 31/07/10

# A IS FOR...

## THE A TO Z OF F1
## YOUR INSTANT REFERENCE GUIDE
## TO FORMULA ONE JARGON...

### A IS FOR AERODYNAMICS

This is the study of airflow over and around an object and is a vital area that influences Formula One car design.

### B IS FOR BALLAST

These are the weights that are fixed around the car to maximise its balance and bring it up to the minimum weight limit – a bit like a jockey riding a horse or a boxer at a weigh-in. It has to be fair to all so similar weights are needed.

### C IS FOR CHASSIS

This is the main part of a racing car which the engine and suspension are attached on to.

### D IS FOR DIFFUSER

You will find the diffuser at the rear section of the car's floor where the air flowing under the car exits. The design of the diffuser is vital to an F1 racing car as it controls the speed at which the air exits – the faster its exit, the lower the air pressure beneath the car, and hence the more down force the car can generate. In simple terms it helps the car go faster.

### E IS FOR ELECTRONIC FUEL INJECTION (EFI)

This is a system that injects fuel into the engine and includes an electronic control unit that times and measures the flow. Fuel is delivered in intermittent pulses by the opening and closing of special fuel injectors.

### F IS FOR FORMATION LAP

This is the lap before the start of the race when the cars are driven round from the grid to assemble on the grid again ready for the start of the race. It is also sometimes referred to as the warm-up lap or parade lap.

### G IS FOR G-FORCE

A word often associated with F1 racing, G-force is a physical force equivalent to one unit of gravity that is multiplied during rapid changes of direction or velocity – but you knew that already! Drivers can experience severe G-force as they take a corner quickly, accelerate or brake.

### H IS FOR HARD TYRES

A different compound to soft tyres – they last longer but have less grip.

### I IS FOR INSTALLATION LAP

This is a lap (almost) completed on arrival at a circuit where a driver will test vital functions such as throttle, brakes and steering before heading back to the pits - without crossing the finish line.

### J IS FOR JUMP START

This term describes when a driver has moved off his grid position before the five red lights have been switched off to signal the start. Sensors detect premature movement and a jump start earns a driver a penalty – not a good way to begin!

### K IS FOR KERS

KERS stands for Kinetic Energy Recovery Systems – these were made legal in 2009. KERS recover waste kinetic energy from the car during braking, store that energy and then make it available to propel the car – quite clever, really. The driver has access to the additional power for limited periods per lap, via a 'boost button' on the steering wheel – a bit like having a computer game controller on hand to give the car that extra va-va-voom!

### L IS FOR LOLLIPOP

This is the sign on a stick held in front of the car during a pit stop to tell the driver to apply the brakes and then to engage first gear prior to the car being lowered from its jacks – handy for the pit crew who have just a fraction of a second to get out of the way.

## M IS FOR MARSHAL

This is the guy who ensures the race is run safely. Marshals have many roles to fill, including observing the spectators to ensure they do not endanger themselves or the drivers, acting as fire wardens, helping to remove stranded cars or drivers from the track and using flags to signal the condition of the track to drivers – rarely a job that passes without incident but an interesting one all the same.

## N IS FOR NUMBER PLATE

In 2008, a man paid just over £400,000 for the car registration plate 'F1'!

## O IS FOR OVERSTEER

Oversteer is when the back end of a car attempts to spin round during a fast corner. To correct the problem, the driver needs to opposite-lock, meaning turning the front wheels into the skid.

## P IS FOR PADDOCK

This is an enclosed area behind the pits in which the teams keep their transporters and motor homes. There is no admission to the public, though a few VIPs seem to get in there from time to time!

## Q IS FOR QUALIFYING

This is the knock-out session held on a Saturday during which the drivers compete to set the best time they can in order to determine the starting grid for the race. Needless to say, the fastest gets the pole, the slowest starts at the rear.

## R IS FOR RIDE-HEIGHT

This is the height between the track's surface and the floor of the car – it has to be at the legal distance for safety reasons.

## S IS FOR SHAKEDOWN

It may sound as though it's straight out of an American police movie, but shakedown in F1 is a short test when a team is trying a different car part for the first time before going back out to drive at 100 percent to set a fast time – it basically checks all is working correctly before the driver goes hell-for-leather!

## T IS FOR TEAR-OFF STRIPS

These are the see-through plastic strips that drivers fit to their helmet's visor before the start of the race and then remove as they become dirty – clear vision is crucial when travelling at the speed these guys do.

## U IS FOR UNDERTRAY

This is a separate floor to the car that is bolted onto the underside of the monocoque – bet you wish we'd included monocoque in the A to Z now! That's one you can find out for yourselves!

## V IS FOR VISCOUS

This is a description of a fluid property related to F1 cars meaning thick or sticky.

## W IS FOR WINDSCREEN

Like a normal car in that an F1 car's windscreen is there to protect a driver from wind, rain and flying debris.

## X IS FOR X-RAY

Often needed for drivers involved in high speed bumps or crashes!

## Y IS FOR YAMAHA

Brilliant in many aspects of motor racing, the Japanese constructers found building successful F1 racing cars hard going and never enjoyed a race winner despite numerous attempts.

## Z IS FOR ZOOM LENS

Thousands of high quality photographs are taken during a Grand Prix – close up pictures are taken with expensive zoom lenses.

## SOUTH KOREAN GRAND PRIX
### KOREAN INTERNATIONAL CIRCUIT

**17**

FIRST RACE: 2010
CIRCUIT LENGTH: 5.621 KM
LAPS: 55
BUILT: 2010
CAPACITY: 135,000
RECORD CROWDS: N/A

## SPANISH GRAND PRIX
### CIRCUIT DE CATALUNYA, BARCELONA

**18**

FIRST RACE: 1991
CIRCUIT LENGTH: 4.627 KM
LAPS: 66
LAPS: 50
BUILT: 1991
CAPACITY: 67,730
RECORD CROWD: 2003

## TURKISH GRAND PRIX
**19**
### ISTANBUL PARK CIRCUIT, ISTANBUL
### FIRST RACE: 2005

CIRCUIT LENGTH: 5.34 KM
LAPS: 58
BUILT: 2005
CAPACITY: 155,000
RECORD CROWD: 40,000

# SPOT THE DIFFERENCE

PICTURE A AND B ARE THE SAME – OR ARE THEY? CAN YOU SPOT AND CIRCLE THE SIX DIFFERENCES IN PICTURE B?

Answers on page 60/61

## PEDRO DE LA ROSA

**TEAM:** BMW SAUBER
**BORN:** 24/02/1971
**NATIONALITY:** SPANISH
**BIRTHPLACE:** BARCELONA, SPAIN
**WORLD CHAMPIONSHIPS:** 0
**HIGHEST FINISH:** 2
**RACE WINS:** 0
**TOTAL POINTS:** 29

## NICO ROSBERG

**TEAM:** MERCEDES GP
**BORN:** 27/06/1985
**NATIONALITY:** GERMAN
**BIRTHPLACE:** WIESBADEN, GERMANY
**WORLD CHAMPIONSHIPS:** 0
**HIGHEST FINISH:** 2
**RACE WINS:** 0
**TOTAL POINTS:** 169.5

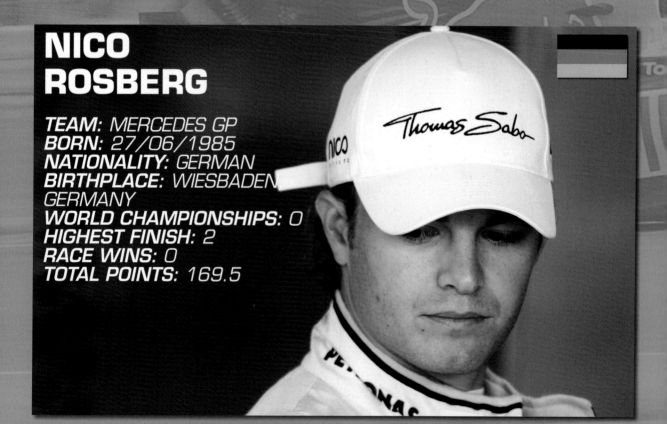

# MICHAEL SCHUMACHER

**TEAM:** *MERCEDES GP*
**BORN:** *03/01/1969*
**NATIONALITY:** *GERMAN*
**BIRTHPLACE:** *HÜRTH-HERMÜLHEIM, GERMANY*
**WORLD CHAMPIONSHIPS:** *7*
**HIGHEST FINISH:** *1*
**RACE WINS:** *91*
**TOTAL POINTS:** *1407*

# BRUNO SENNA

**TEAM:** *HRT*
**BORN:** *15/10/1983*
**NATIONALITY:** *BRAZILIAN*
**BIRTHPLACE:** *SAO PAULO, BRAZIL*
**WORLD CHAMPIONSHIPS:** *0*
**HIGHEST FINISH:** *16*
**RACE WINS:** *0*
**TOTAL POINTS:** *0*

DETAILS CORRECT TO 31/07/10

# ADAYATTHERACETRACK
## THE 2010 BRITISH GRAND PRIX

IT'S ONE OF THE MOST EXCITING DATES ON THE SPORTING
CALENDAR – THE BRITISH GRAND PRIX. THERE WAS ADDED
EXCITEMENT FOR THE 2010 RACE WITH TWO BRITISH DRIVERS AT

THE TOP OF THE DRIVERS' CHAMPIONSHIP – LEWIS HAMILTON AND JENSON BUTTON – AND HUNDREDS OF THOUSANDS OF PEOPLE CAME TO WATCH OVER A SUN-BAKED WEEKEND.

# ADAYATTHERACETRACK
## THE 2010 BRITISH GRAND PRIX

IT DIDN'T QUITE GO ACCORDING TO PLAN WITH AUSSIE MARK
WEBBER WINNING, BUT AT LEAST LEWIS MANAGED SECOND
PLACE ON THE PODIUM. WE'VE CHOSEN PICTURES TO SHOW

WHAT MAKES SILVERSTONE SUCH A SPECIAL DAY FOR THE DRIVERS AND THE RACE FANS WHO FLOCK TO IT. WHO KNOWS, MAYBE YOU'LL BE ONE OF THEM IN 2011!

# DRIVER PROFILES

## ADRIAN SUTIL

**TEAM:** FORCE INDIA
**BORN:** 11/01/1983
**NATIONALITY:** GERMAN
**BIRTHPLACE:** STARNBERG, GERMANY
**WORLD CHAMPIONSHIPS:** 0
**HIGHEST FINISH:** 4
**RACE WINS:** 0
**TOTAL POINTS:** 41

## JARNO TRULLI

**TEAM:** LOTUS
**BORN:** 13/07/1974
**NATIONALITY:** ITALIAN
**BIRTHPLACE:** PESCARA, ITALY
**WORLD CHAMPIONSHIPS:** 0
**HIGHEST FINISH:** 1
**RACE WINS:** 1
**TOTAL POINTS:** 246.5

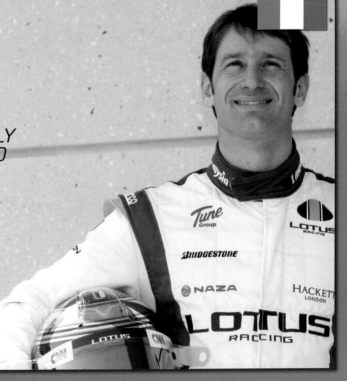

# SEBASTIAN VETTEL

**TEAM:** RED BULL RACING
**BORN:** 03/07/1987
**NATIONALITY:** GERMAN
**BIRTHPLACE:** HEPPENHEIM, GERMANY
**WORLD CHAMPIONSHIPS:** 0
**HIGHEST FINISH:** 1
**RACE WINS:** 7
**TOTAL POINTS:** 261

# MARK WEBBER

**TEAM:** RED BULL RACING
**BORN:** 27/08/1976
**NATIONALITY:** AUSTRALIAN
**BIRTHPLACE:** QUEANBEYAN, AUSTRALIA
**WORLD CHAMPIONSHIPS:** 0
**HIGHEST FINISH:** 1
**RACE WINS:** 5
**TOTAL POINTS:** 305.5

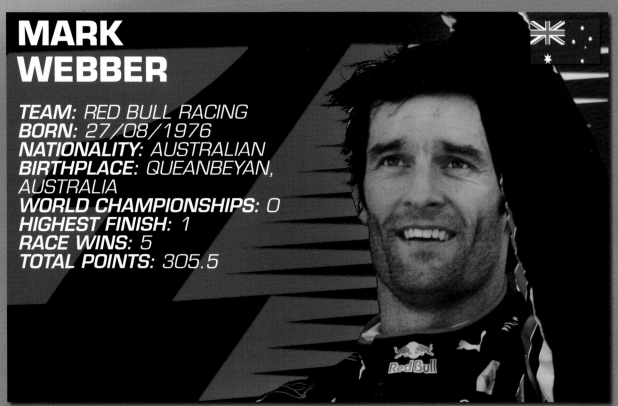

# CHAMPIONS ROLL OF HONOUR

HERE IS A LIST OF THE CHAMPION DRIVERS WHO, OVER THE COURSE OF THE F1 SEASON, PROVED THEY WERE THE BEST...

| YEAR | CHAMPIONS | CONSTRUCTORS |
|---|---|---|
| 2009 | Jenson BUTTON (GBR) | Brawn-Mercedes |
| 2008 | Lewis HAMILTON (GBR) | Mercedes |
| 2007 | Kimi RAIKKONEN (FIN) | Ferrari |
| 2006 | Fernando ALONSO (SPA) | Renault |
| 2005 | Fernando ALONSO (SPA) | Renault |
| 2004 | Michael SCHUMACHER (GER) | Ferrari |
| 2003 | Michael SCHUMACHER (GER) | Ferrari |
| 2002 | Michael SCHUMACHER (GER) | Ferrari |
| 2001 | Michael SCHUMACHER (GER) | Ferrari |
| 2000 | Michael SCHUMACHER (GER) | Ferrari |
| 1999 | Mika HAKKINEN (FIN) | Ferrari |
| 1998 | Mika HAKKINEN (FIN) | McLaren - Mercedes |
| 1997 | Jacques VILLENEUVE (CAN) | Williams - Renault |
| 1996 | Damon HILL (GBR) | Williams - Renault |
| 1995 | Michael SCHUMACHER (GER) | Benetton - Renault |
| 1994 | Michael SCHUMACHER (GER) | Williams - Renault |
| 1993 | Alain PROST (FRA) | Williams - Renault |
| 1992 | Nigel MANSELL (GBR) | Williams - Renault |
| 1991 | Ayrton SENNA (BRA) | McLaren - Honda |
| 1990 | Ayrton SENNA (BRA) | McLaren - Honda |
| 1989 | Alain PROST (FRA) | McLaren - Honda |
| 1988 | Ayrton SENNA (BRA) | McLaren - Honda |
| 1987 | Nelson PIQUET (BRA) | Williams - Honda |
| 1986 | Alain PROST (FRA) | Williams - Honda |
| 1985 | Alain PROST (FRA) | McLaren - TAG/Porsche |
| 1984 | Niki LAUDA (AUT) | McLaren - TAG/Porsche |

| 1983 | Nelson PIQUET (BRA) | Ferrari |
| 1982 | Keke ROSBERG (FIN) | Ferrari |
| 1981 | Nelson PIQUET (BRA) | Williams - Ford/Cosworth |
| 1980 | Alan JONES (AUS) | Williams - Ford/Cosworth |
| 1979 | Jody SCHECKTER (SAF) | Ferrari |
| 1978 | Mario ANDRETTI (USA) | Lotus - Ford/Cosworth |
| 1977 | Niki LAUDA (AUT) | Ferrari |
| 1976 | James HUNT (GBR) | Ferrari |
| 1975 | Niki LAUDA (AUT) | Ferrari |
| 1974 | Emerson FITTIPALDI (BRA) | McLaren - Ford/Cosworth |
| 1973 | Jackie STEWART (GBR) | Lotus - Ford/Cosworth |
| 1972 | Emerson FITTIPALDI (BRA) | Lotus - Ford/Cosworth |
| 1971 | Jackie STEWART (GBR) | Tyrrell - Ford/Cosworth |
| 1970 | Jochen RINDT (AUT) | Lotus - Ford/Cosworth |
| 1969 | Jackie STEWART (GBR) | Matra - Ford/Cosworth |
| 1968 | Graham HILL (GBR) | Lotus - Ford/Cosworth |
| 1967 | Denny HULME (NZL) | Brabham - Repco |
| 1966 | Jack BRABHAM (AUS) | Brabham - Repco |
| 1965 | Jim CLARK (GBR) | Lotus - Climax |
| 1964 | John SURTEES (GBR) | Ferrari |
| 1963 | Jim CLARK (GBR) | Lotus - Climax |
| 1962 | Graham HILL (GBR) | BRM |
| 1961 | Phil HILL (USA) | Ferrari |
| 1960 | Jack BRABHAM (AUS) | Cooper - Climax |
| 1959 | Jack BRABHAM (AUS) | Cooper - Climax |
| 1958 | Mike HAWTHORN (GBR) | Vanwall |
| 1957 | Juan Manuel FANGIO (ARG) | Independent |
| 1956 | Juan Manuel FANGIO (ARG) | Independent |
| 1955 | Juan Manuel FANGIO (ARG) | Independent |
| 1954 | Juan Manuel FANGIO (ARG) | Independent |
| 1953 | Alberto ASCARI (ITA) | Independent |
| 1952 | Alberto ASCARI (ITA) | Independent |
| 1951 | Juan Manuel FANGIO (ARG) | Independent |
| 1950 | Giuseppe 'Nino' FARINA (ITA) | Independent |

# QUIZANSWERS

## FIND JENSON ANSWERS (PG 34)

## SPOT THE DIFFERENCE ANSWERS (PG 16)
The differences are circled

## SPOT THE DIFFERENCE ANSWERS (PG 49)
The differences are circled

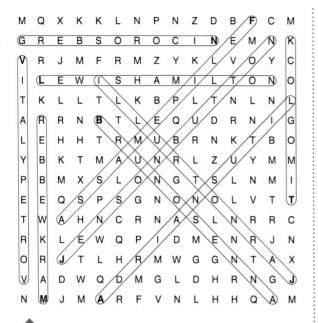

**WORDSEARCH SOLUTION (PG 33)**

**CROSSWORD SOLUTION (PG 25)**

# THEBIG
# F1 QUIZ
### ANSWERS FROM (PG 40)

01, NICO HULKENBERG
02, MARK WEBBER
03, MICHAEL SCHUMACHER,
   NICO ROSBERG, ADRIAN SUTIL,
   TIMO GLOCK, NICO HULKENBERG
04, RACE MARSHAL
05, BRAWN-GP
06, RUSSIA
07, SEVEN
08, CANADIAN AND FRENCH GPS
09, BAHRAIN
10, JENSON BUTTON
11, BOTH HAVE STREET CIRCUITS
12, FELIPE MASSA
13, IT WAS THE 60TH ANNIVERSARY OF F1
   GRAND PRIX
14, NICO ROSBERG
15, FERNANDO ALONSO
16, SECOND
17, TWO
18, FERRARI
19, SEBASTIAN VETTEL
20, B) 2006

**WHICH CIRCUIT?**
**ANSWERS (PG 42)**

A, MONACO
B, BAHRAIN
C, CANADA
D, VALENCIA,
SPAIN

**GUESS WHO?**
**ANSWERS (PG 20)**

1, Mark Webber

2, Fernando Alonso

3, Sebastian Vettel

4, Jenson Button

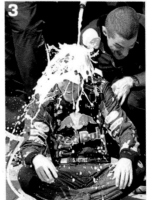

page61